Cover Design: Gordon Robertson
Cover Illustration: 'Closed System' by Gail Geltner
Printed in Canada

COACH HOUSE PRESS
401 (rear) Huron Street
Toronto, Canada
M5S 2G5

COUNSELLING IN THE WORKPLACE

Adrian Coles

OPEN UNIVERSITY PRESS

Open University Press
McGraw-Hill Education
McGraw-Hill House
Shoppenhangers Road
Maidenhead
Berkshire
England
SL6 2QL

email: enquiries@openup.co.uk
world wide web: www.openup.co.uk

First published 2003

A catalogue record of this book is available from the British Library

ISBN 0 335 21211 5

Library of Congress Cataloging-in-Publication Data
CIP data has been applied for

Typeset by RefineCatch Limited, Bungay, Suffolk
Printed in Great Britain by MPG Books Ltd, Bodmin, Cornwall

In memory of Sheila Overton

For Tricia, Chloe and Oscar

Contents

Series editors' preface   ix
Preface   xi
Acknowledgements   xiii

1 · THE DEVELOPMENT OF COUNSELLING IN THE
    WORKPLACE   1

2 · THE CONTEXT OF WORKPLACE COUNSELLING   26

3 · THE PRACTICE OF COUNSELLING AT WORK   47

4 · SPECIFIC ISSUES IN WORKPLACE COUNSELLING   77

5 · PROFESSIONAL RELATIONSHIPS IN COUNSELLING
    IN THE WORKPLACE   94

6 · A CRITIQUE OF COUNSELLING IN THE WORKPLACE   122

Appendix I   138
Appendix II   143
References   145
Index   151

Series editors' preface

Work dominates our lives, particularly in Britain where it appears we work the longest hours of all. Freud indeed summed up the aim of adult life as 'to love and to work', although he paid far less attention to work than he did to love. And this has been generally true of the development of psychotherapy and counselling – it has concentrated on relationships, largely those of the family and the home, and has by and large ignored the dynamics of work and work relationships, which form a major part of most people's daily lives. People probably spend more time relating to colleagues than they do to their partners and children and, if we take away the sleeping hours, they probably spend as much time at work as they do in their homes. Intimate relationships are often formed through people meeting at work, and the absence of work with redundancy or retirement has a major impact on psychological health.

There have been some exceptions to this lack of interest in work, mainly from the organizational perspective, where such studies as those conducted by the Tavistock Institute of Human Relations have informed those in management positions of some of the dynamics of the workplace. But, as with the development of psychotherapy itself, the benefits of the psychological study of the workplace initially were only available to the privileged and the few.

As Adrian Coles shows, some of the privileged did care about their workforce, pioneering health and social welfare in their factories, with a concern that came we may suspect as much from charitable conviction as from the desire to keep production going. Whether that is the same today, with the increase in employee assistance programmes (EAPs), we cannot tell, although we suspect that the way they are sold is as much on the basis of keeping staff productive at work as in the interests of their well-being outside work. Undeniably, however, the rapid increase of provision of counselling in the workplace has brought some of the benefits of therapy to the workforce at all levels, albeit for those who still cannot afford therapy, in the same limited form that we see in primary care and even now in universities and colleges.

Workplace counselling has arrived somewhat late on the scene – and in this series – but it has rapidly overtaken some other settings both in its spread and in the research findings into its benefits. John McLeod's collation of research has shown that counselling reduces levels of stress, that sickness and absence fall significantly, that job commitment and satisfaction rise, and that successful results are achieved even with the small number of sessions that can usually be offered. Brief work may therefore be driven forward for financial reasons, but nonetheless it confirms what is found in other settings – that much can be given by fewer sessions to many, and not, as some long-standing myths would have it, that much can only be given by many sessions to the few.

There is another reason why workplace counselling is important beyond the confines of the workplace. Not only are more counsellors and therapists in independent practice working for EAPs and therefore can benefit from this study of counselling in the workplace – with the emphasis here on the workplace itself – but counsellors and therapists, wherever they work, inevitably find themselves listening to narratives about the working life and the work setting of many of their clients. Given what we have said in the first paragraph, the workplace is a very significant part of a person's world, and while it may appear to be 'outside' and distant from the therapeutic relationship, in fact some of their inner processes are sure to reflect in the person's relationship to work; and without doubt their working life impinges significantly upon their relationships in the home and at leisure. Like work itself, the lessons from this book spread beyond the book's immediate context.

Moira Walker
Michael Jacobs

Preface

I have always been interested in work, especially why we do it, how we do it and how we manage to spend so long in the company of our work colleagues. My early interest in work was greatly expanded by learning some of Karl Marx's theories about work. This helped me to develop an economic understanding of why we work. A deeper psychological understanding of why we work came later when I started to read Sigmund Freud's writings about our internal worlds. Our postmodern working lives involve the basic economic and profound psychological concepts that Marx and Freud developed for us. Counselling in the workplace involves a combination of economic and psychological factors of which all counsellors entering into this setting need to have a firm understanding.

This book is not about how to practise workplace counselling, although there is an element of operational detail in some of the chapters. It is aimed at exploring *why* we find counselling in the workplace, at this point in time, in the particular forms that it takes, and *why* it is found in our postmodern organizations. *Why* has the concept of counselling moved from private counselling rooms to the shop floor, boardroom and offices of private and public sector organizations?

The main theories and practices that have formed my views on counselling in the workplace are psychodynamic and sometimes specifically Freudian. However, I have used other theories and listened to many others. Freudian theory alone is not useful to the many managers and employees to whom I have talked about their organizations and counselling services that they have developed or introduced. I have been influenced by systemic theories in particular, as most employees readily talk about their working lives as being part of a group or not part of a group, and how there are almost always other employees in an organization, or outside of an organization, who can be blamed for their woes.

The other main influences on my work have been from Gerry Egan, Michael Reddy and Michael Carroll: Egan initially for his ideas about helping individuals, and later for applying sophisticated processes to helping managers and organizations; Reddy, for the application of his ideas which have led to the growth of a company that has provided a 'benchmark' for me in looking at why some things are done in certain ways; and Carroll because I consider his two books on workplace counselling to be the primary texts to date describing the workplace counselling setting in this country. All three of them have helped me with warmth and kindness in sharing their knowledge with me. None of them would describe themselves as Freudians.

This book is not a research document. My ideas about the management of counsellors and counselling organizations are products developed from listening to and interviewing many employees, counsellors, psychologists, psychotherapists and counsellor managers. What I have tried to do is to put some of their ideas together and take some of their concepts further. I am grateful to them all for giving their time to further my own study of this setting.

Acknowledgements

Many people have helped me to write this book. Some of them have inspired me, some have provided information and some have shared their hopes and fears with me about workplace counselling. All have given their time and knowledge without question, patiently and graciously. Without their cooperation, this book would have remained an opinion.

Gerry Egan, Michael Reddy and Michael Carroll have told me about their workplace experiences and shared many of their ideas and thoughts with me, which has helped me to clarify my thinking about the complex issues involved in workplace counselling. Many EAP professionals have assisted me in great depth and explained how they work and what they encounter in the daily routines of their work. In particular, I want to thank Stephen Galliano and Mandy Rutter at ICAS, Angela Clarke at FOCUS, Sandra Ridley at FIRST-ASSIST, Tracey Goodman and Chris Partridge at CREWCARE, Kevin Fiery at Coutts CORECARE and Sue Meehan at Astra Zeneca.

I have been pointed in the right direction by Sylvia Nisenoff (EAPA), Bill Sonnenstuhl, Paul Roman, Paul Steele, Kathryn Hewlett (APA), Rosemary Clough and Brenda Blair. Ava Fine, Colin Grange, Dr Tim Bond and Linda Hoskinson have all contributed by allowing me to talk through some ideas. Trudy Chapman at Guy's Hospital and John Mellor-Clark have been very helpful in providing inspiration for my counsellor manager concepts. Linda Hambelton and Sarah Miller from the Tavistock Consultancy Service have helped me look even further 'below the surface'. A constant source of support and detail has been supplied by Aileen Lee at Hampshire County Council and Helen Fisher, previously at North Staffordshire NHS Trust.

Members of the National Local Authority Counselling Development

Group have also provided huge amounts of detail describing the operation of their services and the problems they encounter.

Other valuble contributions have been from Noreen Tehrani, Lynn Macwhinnie and Professor Wilfred Van de Will. Denise Chaytor at BACP has been helpful with my research and I have used PsychInfo (APA) as a useful reference source. Lesley Davies from Bootshelp, and Elizabeth Grayson and Roberta Crossland from Northamptonshire Police have all given me their time and stories about the development of their services.

Shirley Cully helped me with the early history of workplace counselling organizations and Barry McInnes spoke to me about the ACW. Discussions at the EAPA UK executive have been an inspiration, and I have been glad to be able to work alongside them as they develop their professional body. My supervisees have given me further insight into the internal worlds of various organizations.

Many managers, employees, headteachers, trade union officials, personnel professionals and others at Northamptonshire County Council have helped me develop my ideas in the workplace and reflecting on this has helped me write this book.

Michael Jacobs has been a kind and constructive editor and Cathy Thompson at Open University Press has waited patiently for the manuscript.

Marianne Phillips, my supervisor, has helped me think through some ideas and Val Roche has continued to listen.

· ONE ·

The development of counselling in the workplace

People's motive for writing history was not objective curiosity but a desire to influence their contemporaries, to encourage and inspire them, or to hold a mirror up before them.
Freud (1919: 83)

The history of counselling in the workplace is not a clear, logical or easy one to determine. It seems to be a story of widely differing pressures ranging from social, political, economic, institutional/ organizational, individual, practitioner and client sources. Some of these pressures may have been conscious, others deeply un-conscious. Whatever these pressures may be, they have led to the present position of counselling in the workplace. In Britain, external employee assistance programmes (EAPs) provide counselling ser-vices for approximately 2.26 million employees, or 10 percent of the working population in 1137 organizations. The value of this business is £22.53 million (EAPA UK 2001). The true figure for employees with access to counselling services is probably much higher than this. In North America the number of organizations using EAPs and coun-selling services accounts for a much higher proportion of the national workforce.

The history of counselling at work also runs parallel to the history of 'work' – and as counselling in the workplace is explored, work and what work means to clients, organizations and counsellors will be examined throughout this book.

HISTORICAL OVERVIEW

Perhaps counselling in the workplace has existed as long as there have been relationships where one person serves another person, in a non-familial context – that is, without a family bond. This idea is based on two major factors; first, the existence of communication between two or more people. Where there is some form of communication there exists the possibility for some level of psychological understanding – which in itself can provide the opportunity for an active psychological interest between the two people. Second, the work relationship, however crude or rudimentary, may require the person in the role of employer to have some interest in the employee in order to maintain the existence of the status of employer/employee, and to maintain the service/labour from which the employer benefits as a direct consequence of the relationship.

A simple version of a relationship between an employer and employee is this: one person takes on a role willingly or unwillingly to provide a service for the other person, the 'other person' having power or control over the 'service provider'. This does not mean that counselling takes this form, or that such a relationship naturally determines that 'counselling' will follow. However, at some point there is some form of communication between these two people, even if it is done through a third party, such as a charge hand, a manager or a union official, even if the communication does not resemble the subtle and sophisticated communications that we understand counselling to be now. There is nothing new in that, and there are many examples in fiction of relationships between employer and employee. Although the relationship in terms of power and control may not be equal, each party has a mutual interest/disinterest in the survival, health and growth of the other. When this interest is healthy and positive, it will contain 'mutuality', that is also an interest in another person – one of the necessary prerequisites for some form of counselling relationship.

Those who have the control and power will at some point take some interest in the welfare of the other, even if it is only to ensure the employee is still able to gratify the desires, needs or appetites of the one in control. Such selfish interests may not seem to be anything like the complex communications and individual interests in work relationships that many people experience today, but actually such communications between the one with power and the one without, are not far removed from many of the work issues that workplace counsellors are presented with every working day.

Employers, even in their most basic form, have for many reasons always needed to have some interest in those that they employ. From primitive, feudal and pre-industrial beginnings, this basic understanding of the relationship between employer/employee has been developed and has undergone many changes, up to our present workplace conditions. In the public sector workplace counselling services are common and access to counselling services is part of the ordinary expectations of employees in much of that sector. The interest that the employer has in a public sector employee may appear to be far more tolerant, benign and sophisticated than a simple interest in maintaining a socioeconomic relationship, but evidence from workplace counsellors counters this assumption: the actual existence of workplace counsellors can be seen to be part of the maintenance of the socioeconomic relationship. These ideas are explored further in the book.

In North America the history of counselling in the workplace appears to be more fully documented than in the UK; perhaps this is because central government in North America has been more actively involved in the last century with the politics of employee care than has central government in Britain. The history of counselling in the workplace in the United Kingdom is less well documented, usually only taking up a couple of pages in the literature (Carroll 1996; Carroll and Walton 1997; Feltham 1997). This suggests that counselling in the workplace has been a gradual evolution, an activity that has grown from practitioners and organizations operating individually, rather than through the coordination of services and practice on a large scale. As I describe in later chapters, this is a reflection of counselling practice – it usually takes place quietly, discreetly and in private. Also some organizations, like many clients who have counselling, may not wish to 'broadcast' the news that they are involved in counselling.

As many practitioners know, in Britain there is still some social stigma attached to being a client receiving counselling. This may be an indication of individual resistance and reluctance to engage in a difficult process, but also social defence mechanisms contribute to the stigma of being a client.

The social position of counselling in the United Kingdom is very different from counselling in other parts of the world, especially in North America, and this is partially due to the access and availability of counselling in the workplace. The more employees have access to workplace counselling in a country, the more 'normal' it appears to be to the wider population. The more government discusses counselling and provides legislation for the access and provision of counselling, the more counselling will be perceived as a part of ordinary work life and, consequently, of life outside of work as well.

DEFINITIONS OF THE 'WORKPLACE' AND 'COUNSELLING'

The specific location of the workplace would appear to have changed radically since the Industrial Revolution, and from the early days of welfare work. Defining the 'workplace' is an interesting problem, but for the present it is enough to indicate how much the workplace seems to have changed for millions of employees and yet how much the workplace has also regressed to very early forms of capitalism. The cottage industries have some similarity to what is often referred to now in many different work sectors, public and private, as 'working from home'. Home was the workplace before and during the Industrial Revolution, and now it is again the workplace for some people as technology advances and another source of stress and anxiety develops.

The British Association of Counselling and Psychotherapy (BACP) has a long-standing definition of counselling, and is probably the most widely accepted version that exists at this time in Britain:

> People become engaged in counselling when a person, occupying regularly or temporarily the role of counsellor offers or agrees explicitly to offer time, attention and respect to another person or persons temporarily in the role of client.
>
> The task of counselling is to give the client an opportunity to explore, discover and clarify ways of living more resourcefully and towards greater well-being.
>
> (BACP 2002)

Further exploration of the application of this definition of counselling in the environment of the workplace, and application of the BACP code of ethics (2002) follows in Chapter 3.

FREUD'S CONCEPT OF WORK

To better understand the historical development of counselling in the workplace, it is necessary to have a basic understanding, first, of some concepts about work and, second, of counselling. Of the many important contributors to the complicated issues of work, I have choosen two: Sigmund Freud and Karl Marx. Freud, although not a prolific writer on work itself (certainly not compared to Marx), explains throughout his development of psychoanalysis what it is to be human. This is important to an understanding of what work means to individuals, groups and organizations. Here Freud explains the need for work:

> No other technique for the conduct of life attaches the individual so firmly to reality as laying emphasis on work; for his work at least gives him a secure place in a portion of reality, in the human community. The possibility it offers of displacing a large amount of libidinal components, whether narcissistic, aggressive or even erotic, on to professional work and on to the human relations connected with it lends it a value by no means second to what it enjoys as something indispensable to the preservation and justification of existence in society.
>
> ([1930] 2001: 268)

Here he describes how work becomes important to ordinary human existence – in particular how other complex psychological processes become attached consciously and unconsciously to what is described as 'work'. Freud was himself a very productive worker, as his first biographer Jones describes: when Freud was busy it 'meant twelve or even thirteen analytic hours in the day' (Jones 1962: 451). And after his regular clinical work Freud would still find time to write. Freud also wrote about our natural aversion of work: 'men [sic] are not spontaneously fond of work' ([1927] 2001: 186).

The majority of people undertake work through necessity and not through choice. Equally, counselling is a task the majority of people undertake through necessity, and not necessarily by choice, although there are obviously differences between the financial necessity of the first and the psychological necessity of the second.

Freud's concepts of the importance of work in a psychological context expand some of Marx's ideas about the alienation of individuals from their sense of self, their relations with other family members and their isolation from larger social groups and communities. Work produces private property at the expense of the individual worker in economic and psychological contexts. It becomes a part of the process of civilization for society, a process that protects society from the natural instincts and urges within all individuals, at the same time as alienating people from themselves and each other. Czander explains the psychoanalytic understanding of work: 'the motivation to control passion and perhaps the wish to manage or to be managed may be the function of a neurotic condition; that is, nothing more than an attempt to blunt the more "shadowy" wishes and motivations for human relatedness and the fears associated with the creative drive to master and accomplish' (1993: 4). Without civilization there would be chaos and destruction, and without work there would be no civilization. Thus, according to Freud's original theory, when we are at work we unconsciously engage in a process that protects us from ourselves and from the needs and desires of others. What a bizarre and strange world the workplace becomes as these ideas are observed and realized.

From my research into the history of workplace counselling, I believe that organizations decide to develop and provide counselling for the workforce often as a consequence of some disaster, tragedy in the workplace or physical/psychological trauma. In this way organizations are no different from individuals seeking psychotherapy or counselling: often as clients or patients we seek help as a result of some external event as well as internal disturbance. Freud ([1921] 2001) explored group psychology and if his concept of the individual and the group psyche is accepted, we can see clearly the parallel between the psychological search for help in an individual and the psychological search for help in an organization. There are other factors that an organization can use to justify its need to search for help – such as economics – in particular the protection of profits and its market interest/position. These large-scale economic factors can influence individual factors in seeking help: if an employee is suffering from a bereavement and seeks counselling for it, the motivation for doing so may well be to maintain their job – to protect their income and employment. Undoubtedly there are some factors that may be unique to organizations that are not applicable to individuals, but following Freud's concept of the psychology of groups being similar to the psychology of the individual, then individual psychology helps us to some extent to understand the organization. Organizations are living, experiencing, conscious/unconscious entities that require help just as any individual does. We are all members of organizations, and as Furnham suggests, we 'are shaped, nurtured, controlled, rewarded and punished by organizations all our lives' (1999: 1).

MARX'S CONCEPT OF WORK

Some years before Freud developed his theories, Karl Marx developed a sophisticated explanation of the capitalist economic systems that evolved with the onset of the Industrial Revolution. Some of Marx's concepts of a 'dynamic psychology came too early to find sufficient attention' (Fromm 1970: 69), and his psychological insight into human life has perhaps been eclipsed by his economic theories. However, Marx describes the 'alienation' (1844: 272) of people from their natural existence through the process of selling their labour to owners of production. Work forces humans to become inhuman as soon as they sell a part of their daily life to someone else for the benefit of the person who buys it. There are four aspects to what Marx describes as 'alienated labour' (1844: 272).

Labour alienates:

1 nature from man;
2 man from himself, makes man passive and brings about self-alienation;
3 man from his own body, nature, his intellect and his human essence;
4 man from other men.

As Marx explains: 'The depreciation of the human world progresses in direct proportion to the increase in the value of the world of things' (McLellan 1972: 134). This concept of alienation is a psychological theory as well as an economic idea, and finds resonance in some of Freud's writing about groups. For example, in order for an individual to belong to a group, he or she has to give up some part of himself or herself to the group. This may be done unconsciously or very overtly, such as through an initiation ceremony or ritual. The part of 'self' that an individual has to abandon makes for some similarity with some of Marx's fundamental facts of alienation.

ALCOHOL: PROGENITOR OF WORKPLACE COUNSELLING

There have been many fashions in the history of employers helping employees. Sonnenstuhl and Trice state:

> Social betterment, personnel counselling, occupational mental health, and industrial alcoholism. Each of these approaches blends management concerns for productivity with humanitarian values – that is, employers believe that helping employees with their troubles increases productivity.
>
> (1995: 3)

At the end of the nineteenth century, some North American companies were providing a variety of services for their workforces such as housing, financial services, recreational facilities, medical care and education. In Britain, there are still many examples of industrial philanthropies in existence. Some of the textile mills in

West Yorkshire, Derbyshire and Lancashire are evidence of benign individual capitalists. These industrialists financed the building of whole self-contained work communities. Sir Titus Salt developed Saltaire, in West Yorkshire, in 1853. This included homes, a huge mill, a school, a chapel and a park. Robert Owen developed New Lanark in Scotland in 1785, and the employees were provided with homes, free healthcare and 'education in a school he called the Institute for the Formation of Character' (Ward 2001: 14). New Lanark and Saltaire provided models for further social provision like that at Bournville, Birmingham and Port Sunlight, Wirral. Perhaps now these buildings and the sentiments that led to their construction appear as ideologically grim as they look grimy and bleak from decades of soot, but the workforces were housed, perhaps fed, and certainly supported by the employers. These few employers took some responsibility for their workforce. From a cynical perspective (or from a simple economic perspective) by keeping the worker fit, the capitalist kept his profit fit. How the worker benefited from this patronage is another question, which I return to in Chapter 6.

In North America this philanthropism progressed to providing welfare workers for the workforce. Welfare workers were able to offer comprehensive services to the workforce and to assist with 'social betterment'. Sonnenstuhl and Trice refer to the National Civic Foundation that developed such methods to 'ensure a stable labor force, promote worker loyalty, combat unionism, and prevent strikes' (1995: 3). However, with the increasing strength of the trade unions and American labour organizations, workers became disillusioned with these services. This disillusion led to violent conflict between the emerging trade unions and the company owners. Consequently managers had to develop quickly and experiment with a wide range of managerial techniques and concepts to maintain production and hold on to the workforce. Sonnenstuhl (1986: 4) states that from 1880 to 1936 'social Darwinism, scientific management, social welfarism, and human relations' were management concepts that were utilized to manipulate and maintain relationships with workforces. Each of these methods had merits, but also had problems. Briefly, social Darwinism introduced the concept of the fittest surviving in the workplace – the fittest being managers and productive workers. This idea was slightly modified but did little to assist the difficulties between workers and managers. Scientific management, or 'Taylorism' (named after F.W. Taylors' (1911) book), suggested that

> workers are motivated by money – the more discrete the tasks,
> the easier the work, the more productivity, and the more money

for labor and management. The cause of unsatisfactory performance is either poorly defined tasks or 'bad' employees. If poorly defined tasks and rewards cause unsatisfactory performance, management should undertake a scientific study to redefine them more appropriately. If the problem is caused by a bad employee, he or she is fired.

(Sonnenstuhl 1986: 6)

Apparently some of these principles are still to be found in modern management practice. Critics of 'Taylorism' suggest that there is nothing scientific about the concept and that it is just another way of justifying management domination of workers (Sonnenstuhl 1986: 6).

The next management trend was social betterment or social welfarism. This was perhaps a simultaneous development rather than a progression from scientific management, and evolved mainly from the paternalistic attitudes of industrialists like Henry Boot, Rowntree and Cadbury. Welfarism developed mainly in Europe, and an example is provided below in the brief history of Bootshelp. One of the main differences between welfarism and scientific management is the environment(s) in which these concepts and practices developed. As Sonnenstuhl (1986: 7) points out, welfarism developed in industries like retail stores and textile mills because the workforces were predominantly women workers, and often geographically isolated – the Saltaire scheme in West Yorkshire was built around the mill. Scientific management developed in urban industries mainly populated by a male workforce. Welfarism is quite a simple principle designed to *keep* the workforce, and to reduce the need for unionization. Gradually, perceptions of how much the company owners need to provide for employees has changed, and scientific management and welfarism principles have combined in the evolution of personnel administration functions (Sonnenstuhl 1986: 8).

During the 1930s, as the trades union movement became stronger, companies around the world started to drop many of their welfarism programmes and the next managerial fashion was to develop 'human relations'. The main influence was Elton Mayo, who suggested companies should have their own psychiatric clinics to help workers with their disruptive and abnormal thinking. In other words – mad workers affect profits, so treat the madness in the individual workers using psychiatric interventions and protect the profits. Western Electric helped produce the Hawthorne studies which found that 'work groups, not management, regulated productivity by defining performance standards and by using group pressure to pre-vent rate busting' (Sonnenstuhl 1986: 10). The 'Hawthorne effect' (Sonnenstuhl 1986: 10) was an increase in production created simply by studying the workforce. By listening to and observing the employees at work productivity increased. So the management tried to replicate this by providing a group of employees (not trained coun-sellors) whose function was to offer an individual, confidential listen-ing service to other employees. No actual changes were implemented as a result of these discussions, but Western Electric believed that this policy kept the unions out of the company for about 20 years. This is the basis of the human relations concept and, as Sonnenstuhl suggests, it still has a managerial following, as seen by the number of organizations that refer to their personnel operations as human relations or human resources departments.

Alcohol, and employees' relationships with it, was a major pres-sure that influenced the development of counselling in the work-place in North America, and this coincided with the evolution and development of worldwide capitalism. In Britain, alcohol and the employer's requirement to have a sober workforce was an influence on the history of counselling in the workplace, but it does not seem to have been the catalyst it was in North America. Perhaps this can be explained by some differences in the nature of North American capitalism and British capitalism.

In North America in the mid-1950s, alcoholism and alcohol abuse in the workplace had become such a major problem for employees and employers that a small number of recovering alcoholics were able, over a period of time, to bring about the evolution of job-based alcohol programmes. They eventually had funding and legislation to help them from central government, but there were many difficul-ties, rivalries and splits in the 'social movement' (Steele 1989: 513) that became the modern Employee Assistance Professional Associa-tion (EAPA). The work that individuals did in the mid-1950s with employees may not be what many would call counselling, and there are important distinctions between the employee assistance pro-gramme and counselling of employees, which will be examined in Chapter 6. However, without the energy, enthusiasm and anti-alcoholic zeal that many of these early pioneers displayed, perhaps counselling in the workplace would be very different today. It was predominantly the work of Alcoholics Anonymous (AA) that inspired the individuals in North America, eventually leading to the formation of the Association of Labor-Management Administrators and Consultants on Alcohol (ALMACA) in 1971. This group was supported by two other large groups, the National Council on

Alcoholism (NCA) and the National Institute on Alcohol Abuse and Alcoholism (NIAAA). The job-based alcohol programmes in the early 1970s comprised the following elements – 'a written policy statement, focused on employees with alcohol dependence and emphasized the role of the supervisor in the secondary prevention of alcohol related problems through constructive confrontation' (Steele and Trice 1995: 398).

These programmes were active and directive. They involved the line managers/supervisors in the treatment of individual workers. From the early 1970s, the number of job-based programmes increased and became more diverse and complex. Employee assistance programmes developed in a different form from the early alcohol systems, as they included self-referral by employees, the use of external agencies for treatment and a 'broad brush' approach to the variety of problems that could affect an employee's performance, such as financial, familial, disciplinary matters and so on (Steele 1989: 521).

Rosemary Clough discovered that there were quite different approaches to workplace alcohol management in Britain and North America. She was a 'company counsellor' at Control Data, a computer firm with offices in various parts of Britain. The parent company in Minneapolis had a well-established EAP. The company's main concerns were employee welfare, alcoholism and the strength of the trade unions at that time. She received training in the US, but learnt that dealing with an employee's alcohol problem in the US was quite different to how it was dealt with in Britain. In North America, trade unions expected their members to be given all possible help and treatment when alcoholism was recognized, and thus the employee's job was protected as they received treatment. In Britain, Clough found that management and unions unknowingly tended to do the opposite – they would protect an employee from having their alcoholism identified, which eventually would lead to employees losing their jobs when the problem could no longer be concealed.

WELFARE TO COUNSELLING

Many organizations provided 'welfare' for their employees, and gradually some welfare functions evolved into modern personnel management, human resources or counselling services. The first professional welfare worker was Mary Wood, who started her welfare career at Rowntrees in 1896. In June 1913, the Welfare Worker's Association (WWA) was formed and this represented about 60 welfare workers in British industry, including four workers at the Boots Company. The WWA later became the Institute of Personnel Management (IPM).

The history of welfare provision in several large organizations is useful as a description of the evolution of workplace counselling services.

The Boots Company

The growth of services for employees in the Boots Company is a good example of a large number of different pressures and factors that influence creative methods of helping employees and profits simultaneously. This internal counselling service has an interesting pedigree and history, evolving from the benign paternalism of Sir Jesse Boot.

The Boots Company employed a part-time 'welfare officer' from 1891 to 1903, Clara Heath, and she was provided with a bicycle in 1893 so that she could visit women employees who were ill or in situations of hardship. At this early stage in the history of the company, the care of employees was strictly demarcated along gender lines – Jesse Boot took responsibility for the 'welfare' of all the male managers and employees, and his wife Florence took responsibility for the female employees. Florence's 'welfare' role included serving cups of coffee and hot chocolate to women employees as they arrived for work in the mornings.

In 1903 Clara Heath left the company because she got married – another indicator of the context in which these early services were being developed, a paternalistic, perhaps chauvinistic, rigid class and gender system. The next welfare officer, Eleanor Kelly, took over in 1911, by which time there were over 1000 female employees in the 40 Nottingham factories, and many more in the retail sites. Born in 1884 and brought up in New York and England, she had trained as a social worker, and her first job was as a 'welfare worker' for a tin box manufacturer, Hudson Scotts. Here she made a positive contribution to the health and safety of the female employees by introducing basins with hot water, soap and towels in some of the workrooms. The women were working on heavy metal presses, up to their elbows in grease without washrooms or lavatories, and in her first week Eleanor Kelly realized that some of the women had lost fingers and thumbs on the presses. There were no first aid facilities or sick rooms. Florence Boot visited this factory, met Eleanor Kelly and persuaded her to visit the Boots factories and to stay at the family mansion. Here

Jesse Boot encouraged Kelly to move to Nottingham and help with the care of the female employees at Boots. The Boots factories and the tasks of the female workers in the factories were not as dangerous or as foreboding as the work in the tin box manufacturer's, and so Kelly's objectives were not as radical. However, she secured some important changes: renovation of the staff canteen and a sick room next to her office which employed a full-time nurse and doctor. Kelly helped implement 'record cards' for all female employees, and gradually expanded her role to visiting female employees each afternoon, to help them access other forms of assistance such as the Salvation Army or church help. Sometimes these 'referrals' would come from Jesse Boot directly. Kelly required help in her role and so recruited two trained social workers, Agatha Harrison and Miss Kerr, as well as a physical education teacher, Miss Holme. She also sought help from other 'welfare workers'.

The welfare workers at Boots continued helping the workforce, and their presence in the company brought other innovations, such as social benefits, salary administration and sickness leave. In 1920 when the Retail Staff Department was developed, the manager of this department was given the responsibility for wage claims, workers' grievances and negotiations with trade unions. In the 1950s the number of welfare officers increased.

The decision to provide workplace counselling seems to have followed two employee suicides that happened in the Boots Company in the early 1980s. The head of personnel at that point decided that some form of counselling was required for employees. This is perhaps the main critical event that encouraged the organization to seek counselling help.

Now the Bootshelp Service employs nine counsellors, with two other self-employed counsellors, across the United Kingdom and Irish Republic. The roles of the current counsellors, recruited from predominantly social work backgrounds complemented by professional formal counselling training, include other functions in the workplace as well as traditional, individual counselling. Currently, the Boots Company offers this counselling service to its 100,000 employees, 19,900 of whom are retired staff. It is an interesting internal service that combines a number of roles for staff and management. In many ways, it features the services found within traditional EAPs – advice, guidance, employment law information and so on, as well as individual counselling. It exists in a predominantly non-union context – although some areas of the business are unionized. It thus provides a function as the employee's 'voice' in some instances, for example, the head of the Bootshelp Service has attended employment tribunals against the company, representing an employee.

The Post Office

Noreen Tehrani's account of her experience in the Post Office (1997: 42) provides an excellent example of how a large public sector organization – with up to 200,000 employees – can provide an effective and trustworthy internal counselling service. She also shows how the service had to change to meet the needs and demands of the organization's business, and the needs and demands of the employees. This is an example of internal 'political' pressures within an organization, the needs of welfare workers in the organization and recognition of the appropriate style of assistance that employees actually require. All of these factors contributed to the innovation of the counselling service in the Post Office.

The history of welfare provision in the Post Office runs parallel to the development of welfare services in Britain. After the Second World War, as the government developed schemes and services for the working and non-working population, organizations did not have to provide as much care for the employees and their families as they had done previously. The role of welfare officers in the workplace changed, although, as Tehrani points out, there are still some traditional varieties of welfare services still to be found in Britain. But one of the new problems that welfare officers were expected to help employees with was *stress*. Definitions of stress are complex and varied; however, in the Post Office, Tehrani states, 'as a result of the Post Office's caring culture and the support provided to employees the levels of stress experienced by Post Office employees are generally less than those found in other organisations' (1997: 44).

The Post Office Welfare Service has a long and successful history, and decided to change its name to Employee Support on its fiftieth anniversary in May 1995. This followed a rigorous exploration and report into the welfare service. One of the main findings about the welfare service was that 'although the service was valued, it lacked a business focus which was vital to the development of an effective customer–supplier relationship' (Tehrani 1997: 47). Up until this time measuring effectiveness had been limited to measuring the amount of time taken by a welfare officer to help the employee. Tehrani suggested that this meant the focus of the work from the welfare officer's perspective was primarily based on time rather than on results or problems solved. Thus, the welfare officers had an economic interest in maintaining the relationship with the employee. This was unsatisfactory for all concerned. When Tehrani took over in October 1994, it was apparent 'that in order to help the organisation meet its moral and legal obligations to employees, Welfare had to be a more broadly based and professionally qualified service' (1997: 47).

The legal and moral obligation an organization has towards its employees raises some interesting and complex questions about principles. Tehrani suggests that there are three types of care that an organization owes to the employees.

First, there is the duty of care that is defined in the legal structures of employment law in Britain. Second, 'organisational mission and values' (Tehrani 1997: 49) can be translated to mean that an organization believes it can help reduce mental health problems in the workforce by providing a workplace that does not contribute to employee mental health problems, through clarity about job role and counselling services for employees. Third, 'individual effectiveness' (Tehrani 1997: 49) – a concept that makes a philosophical/ sociopolitical assumption – is a particular activity that an organization can provide, mainly focused on helping the individual employee maximize their efficiency and thus help the organization maximize its efficiency. A variety of services may be provided to assist employees achieve this, such as information, advice, problem identification and counselling.

However, as Tehrani developed her role in the Post Office she realized that regarding the

> changing needs of the organization for support in the psychosocial area of employee well-being, there had to be a change in the emphasis of the welfare service from one which had its main focus on social issues to one which also embraced psychological aspects of employee well-being.
>
> (1997: 49)

It was apparent that another system was required to meet the increase in psychological issues that were being recognized by the Employee Support advisors, the management and the organization. Tehrani believed that a psychological service was required that would have to meet the needs of the organization and not the other way around. She observed that at that time many organizations had counselling services, but they appeared to be minor modifications of private practice counselling models. Tehrani wanted to establish a counselling service that met the various needs of the organization and would reflect the organizational setting, rather than set up another in-house private counselling practice. My understanding is that Tehrani needed to develop a system that was not a service that perpetuated itself and its own socioeconomic needs. There are still plenty of services such as those she observed. The employees are undoubtedly assisted by some of these counselling provisions, but the main reason for the existence of some of these services is for the profit of the counsellors involved, not that of the organization funding the counselling service.

Tehrani wanted a counselling system that fitted the organization, not an organization that fitted a private practice counselling system. So she developed First Line Counselling (1997: 52), which has a very clearly defined set of objectives, values and structures. There is a limit of four sessions per employee. Tehrani outlines the stages that are included in this solution-focused method of working. The model is viewed by Tehrani as a product, and as such it can be measured, evaluated and improved. Tehrani sums up her approach and her attempt to rationalize an internal workplace counselling service: 'the client is *always* the organisation' (unpublished interview, 2001).

The evolution of Employee Support into First Line Counselling followed a general social trend towards the need for psychological help for employees from professionals at work, but it also developed from the 'business values' brought in by Tehrani. This is an interesting combination that sometimes worries more traditional counselling practitioners. Some of the pioneers referred to later in this chapter have been in key positions in the history of counselling in the workplace, and have combined other values with traditional counselling practice.

Other organizations have shown that they believe very strongly in the benefits of a counselling service. The reasons for developing such services have some common factors. The following examples of contemporary workplace counselling services demonstrate these, and highlight several other relevant factors in the history of counselling in the workplace.

Northamptonshire Constabulary

The national critical event that spurred on the development of a staff counselling service in the Northamptonshire police force was the Bradford fire in 1984. Prior to it, the force had offered support mainly to police pensioners and to relatives of officers who died on duty. This was done through the medical officer and the Police Federation. The Federation has a long history of advice and assistance in the police services around the country. Following the fire, the Northampton-shire force experimented with a peer counselling system and a separate employee assistance programme, both of which have been replaced by an internal system that provides a holistic approach to employee care and is managed by Elizabeth Grayson, in the Occupational Health Safety and Welfare Department. Grayson, a nurse who was also a trained counsellor, joined the welfare team in 1988. Recognizing the counselling needs of the workforce, she quickly recruited more trained counsellors to cope with the workload. Prior to her arrival, the counselling had been provided by an external counselling organization.

The success of this service was rewarded by an increase in the budget provision. This police force has an employee population of approximately 1400. The service is confidential and now offers brief therapeutic interventions (up to six counselling sessions), the services of eight chaplains and a range of other complementary health specialists, taking a holistic approach to employee well-being.

In the early 1990s two other critical events occurred which influenced the provision of services for the Northamptonshire force employees: the Lockerbie disaster – which directly affected the Lothian Borders police force – and two incidents involving explosives in the Devon and Cornwall Constabulary. These incidents led to the Northamptonshire force adopting a defusing and debriefing policy and practice, to help employees cope with a variety of critical incidents. Now internal force trainers have used a defusing programme with a number of officers to help other employees to deal with the trauma and crises that may occur in their daily duties. The history of this service is quite typical of many public sector organizations – various models and methods are adopted and tried out for a period of time, often to begin with as a reaction to events, but becoming proactive as the individuals employed in welfare and counselling influence the establishment and expansion of the service.

Crewcare

Another typical example of the evolution of an internal counselling system for employees is British Airway's (BA) Crewcare. It is worth noting the development of Crewcare, as it seems to contain most of the elements required for the establishment of an internal counselling system – an initial human crisis, an awareness of contemporary therapeutic practices and human resources practice, and a willingness within the leadership of the organization to assist the workforce and working community.

In 1983 the BA Human Resources Director, Nick Georgeoduous, was aware of a lack of support for the cabin crew community in BA. The realization of this seems to have followed the suicides of two crew members. At that time the cabin crew community was much smaller than it is today. In 1985, Gerard Egan was invited by the Human Resources Director to train a core group of counsellors. Human resources ran a training programme for cabin crew members for about seven years.

There followed financial changes within the organization, and the management of the counselling service changed so that three cabin crew jointly managed the service for a period of time. Later, a stewardess became manager of the service, and two cabin crew were seconded to manage and supervise the counselling team. This service was now called Crewcare and the sole focus was to provide counselling for cabin crew. After extensive research by BA, which included a close look at Work Family Directions in Boston, USA, the counselling provision was put out to tender and Independent Counselling and Advisory Services (ICAS) won the contract for the whole BA workforce.

Crewcare still thrives and still has as its main focus the provision of effective and immediate crisis counselling sessions to any of the 15,000 cabin crew members. The cabin crew are also able to access counselling, advice and information from ICAS if they wish to use this rather than Crewcare. The crisis counselling sessions at present take the form of a single session with a trained cabin crew counsellor. The Egan model (2002) is the main theoretical model that is used to train cabin crew, and a rigorous training programme is undertaken by cabin crew who apply to join the service. In a recent recruitment process, Crewcare had 300 applications from the cabin community to join. Ninety were chosen to attend a two-day selection process of which 13 were recruited to learn the Egan model.

The main success of this service is the integration of the cabin crew into crisis counsellor role within this unique community. Feedback from service users indicates a preference for cabin crew to talk to other cabin crew. A cabin crew 'client' has a list of counsellors to choose from, knowing that all on the list are from the cabin crew community.

Other services that Crewcare offers include a Working Parents Group, that provides seminars for cabin crew thinking of starting a family or returning to work after having children. This is a popular part of their service with substantial uptake. Critical Incident Support for cabin crew is also provided, started after a BA aircraft flew into a flock of geese, causing an engine fire that traumatized some of the crew. Research among other airlines into handling of critical incidents led BA to adopt the Mitchell De-Briefing model, and a tender was put out for a provider. Crewcare writes to any cabin crew involved in a critical incident and offers information on how they can access help, if required.

PIONEERS OF WORKPLACE COUNSELLING

A few individuals stand out as making a singular contribution to development of workplace counselling. These are people who have shaped and developed their own interests in counselling applications to organizational problems, and have consciously and unconsciously determined the development of workplace counselling in the world. Quietly influential and inspirational for many counsellors, managers, clients and employees/employers, these individuals are major forces in the evolution of workplace counselling. Their ideas have helped many counsellors establish their practice within the workplace setting. They have applied a crucial blend of clinical theory and practice with business acumen and commercial awareness. Since it is also these individuals' personalities, anxieties and personal histories that have led them to develop their work and ideas, I include a brief outline of their stories, as a parallel to the history and development of counselling in the workplace.

Michael Reddy

Ask people in the counselling and EAP world who they consider to be a leading figure in the development of counselling in the workplace in the UK, and Michael Reddy's name is always mentioned.

Born in Preston, Lancashire, Reddy realized in his school life that he had an ability to make people laugh, and his sense of performance stayed with him when he studied in a Jesuit seminary and later became a teacher. An interest in psychology took Reddy to the United States where, over six years, he experienced a wide range of therapeutic settings and practices: drop-in centres, student counselling, marriage counselling, physical rehabilitation, alcohol and drug clinics and an intern year in an acute psychiatric unit. Alongside these applications of therapy he explored a variety of other techniques such as bioenergetics, psychodrama, transactional analysis, gestalt and encounter groups. He recognized that he needed to have a sound understanding of one particular form of therapy, and for him this was transactional analysis (TA). His tutor had studied with Fritz Perls as well as Eric Berne, so his teaching was an amalgamation of these two important influences.

After a period of time in South Africa, where Reddy was asked to deliver some counselling training, he returned to Europe and took his final exams in TA. He went on to play a hugely influential role 'in the establishment of TA in the rest of Europe and in the formation of the European Association for Transactional Analysis (EATA)' (Parlett and Page 1990: 200).

A managing director of a brewing company asked him to run a TA course and this turned into a ten-year project, including training courses such as people management, negotiating skills, interpersonal skills and finally counselling skills, for the whole range of the workforce: sales, line managers, human resources, welfare and occupational health.

Reddy gathered together a small team of people with a variety of skills to meet some of these demands and formed a small business: Independent Counselling and Advisory Services (ICAS). Today this company is much bigger than he ever intended it to be, although now he has no operational responsibilities in it. He takes pride in the beliefs of ICAS, which remain simple and effective: 'help for the individual, projected and magnified on the screen of the whole organisation'. He handles employees with whom organizations do not know how to work, as he can relate to the contextual workplace and hierarchy issues to do this. This relates back to his earlier work with individuals, although now he is working with individuals who have a large impact on the efficiency and effectiveness of organizations.

Gerard Egan

Egan is well known among counsellors for the 'Three Stage Model' he introduced in his major work *The Skilled Helper* (2002). He deserves to be included as a pioneer of counselling at work, not only because of his accessible theoretical contribution but because of his application of his theories to the tasks of management.

I recall his description of his approach to a consultancy project he had taken on for a large American retailer. He entered one of the company stores – he walked in just like any other customer would, and started casually to observe what was happening in that store: the way staff spoke to customers and the way that staff spoke to each other. From these preliminary observations he was able to build a picture of what it was like to shop at that store, and he gained some idea of what it might be like to work there. This simple idea about casual observation of people at work in their work environment and talking their work language is a crucial part of understanding the significant contextual structures of a particular workplace. Without an understanding of what employees do and how employees go about their tasks the counsellor in the workplace will limit their effectiveness. Egan's observations raise an important issue for workplace counsellors – how well do they know the organization and the everyday culture that the employees, and their clients, inhabit?

Egan's book, *The Skilled Helper* (2002), reputedly the world's most widely used counselling training text, was first published in 1975 and is now in its seventh edition. It provides a complete practical working model for helping individuals in a one-to-one scenario, which can be translated easily and applied to helping small and large groups. The 'Three Stage Model' is a description of a process that can be adapted and integrated with many theoretical principles. The first stage is about the client's story – this could be compared to psychodynamic notions of the unconscious, and the material of the psyche that lies underneath all thoughts, emotions and actions. From a cognitive-behavioural perspective, the model offers a simple frame for rational and logical exploration of a problem. From a humanistic perspective the model offers a simple structure to explore the here and now, and to facilitate movement led by the client. Some of his later work such as *Adding Value* (1993) is an extension of the Three Stage Model into a systematic model for developing management and leadership in organizations. It includes many examples of his managerial consultancy experiences: 'all bases have to covered' means attending to every eventuality and detail. Every possible turn an organization could take needs to be considered. An effective consultant entering an organization uses similar methods and processes to a counsellor, with a keen interest in the detail of a client's words and movements. The organization is a living, breathing conscious and unconscious entity and deserves this attention from a managerial consultant or workplace counsellor.

Born in 1930 to Irish immigrant parents in Chicago and educated at a Jesuit seminary, Egan started out as a philosophy teacher, until he became more interested in psychology and started an MA programme in clinical psychology. He was ordained as a priest in 1965, and was soon asked to teach psychology in the seminary. He undertook his doctorate in clinical psychology at Loyola University, Chicago, and was asked to stay on and develop an MA programme in counselling psychology, which he did for about 12 years.

He became convinced that many individuals have problems in everyday living because of their social settings rather than because of tormented internal psychic struggles. His first writing was about the impact that larger social settings and social structures, like culture, have upon individuals. His early interest in the social context has remained a theme throughout his work, and he spends much of his time as 'counsel to management', helping organizations to develop more humane and professional management practices 'to produce a management system that is both productive and humane' (Egan 2001). He sees himself as the provider of what he calls 'the four C's: consultant, coach, counsellor and confidante for managers'.

Michael Carroll

Michael Carroll, born in Belfast in 1945, started his professional career, similarly, as a priest. He became interested in counselling and completed the Egan programme at Loyola University, Chicago, obtaining his MA in counselling psychology. On his return to the United Kingdom he spent the next seven years establishing training programmes for social workers and psychologists in counselling, and helped to develop a counselling centre in Glasgow, later moving to London and to a lectureship in counselling at the Roehampton Institute, where he stayed for ten years.

Carroll became interested in working in organizations during his time at Roehampton – they had a contract with the Metropolitan Police Force to train and supervise their welfare officers. As a result of this he was asked to write and deliver the first diploma in counselling at work. Carroll's publications cover a variety of counselling and organizational issues, such as *The Handbook of Counselling in Organizations* (Carroll and Walton 1997) and *Workplace Counselling* (1996). Since leaving Roehampton he has continued to specialize in management and organizational consultancy, and has been involved in an executive mentoring programme for Premier Prisons.

Reddy and Egan are the grandfathers of contemporary workplace counselling. Carroll has written two important texts on workplace counselling, developing organizational roles for counsellors and taking counselling supervision into the workplace.

Two organizations also require recognition for the work that their members have done in establishing counselling in the workplace over the last 20 years – the Association for Counselling at Work (ACW) and the Employee Assistance Professionals Association UK (EAPA UK).

The Association for Counselling at Work

This organization evolved from two small collections of work-based counsellors joining together, under the umbrella of one of the divisions of the British Association for Counselling and Psychotherapy (BACP). BACP has several divisions to cater for the different needs and requirements of counsellors operating in different contexts and settings, for example, APSCC for pastoral and spiritual care, AUCC for university and college counsellors, and a faculty for counsellors working in primary health care settings. Lynn Macwhinnie and Shirley Cully were two of the many workplace professionals involved in the early development of the ACW. In 1977, the Centre for Professional Employment Counselling (CEPEC) was established and this was primarily concerned with training in work counselling skills and counselling that focused on 'career planning, behavioural difficulties, stress, personal problems and other situations affecting performance at work' (CEPEC 1985). Other areas of CEPEC services included helping redundant executives find employment, assisting graduates select careers, and providing redeployment and retirement information.

In 1984, CEPEC launched CEPEC Managers Counselling Association (CMCA) as a response to the growing demand for counselling skills training from managers. In 1985, CMCA had over 270 members spread throughout the United Kingdom and the following year held a second event with the Counselling At Work Division (CAWD) of the BAC. The CMCA was 'essentially for Managers using counselling skills'(CMCA 1987). The CMCA and CAWD joined together to form the ACW under the chair of Judith Baron.

Today, the ACW is looking forward to the expansion of workplace counselling. Although perceived predominantly as 'a counsellors' club' by non-counsellors, the ACW has a mixed professional membership. The speakers attending their annual conferences reflect the membership; the speakers at the 1999 ACW conference included Michael Palin (the writer and actor), the director of personnel at Boots, directors from two other large private companies, a senior university lecturer and the chair of the New Opportunities Fund.

One of the exciting possibilities for the future expansion of the ACW is the prospect of combining resources with the EAPA

UK. This could lead to joint workplace counselling training projects, accreditation and mutual exchanging of resources and interests.

The Employee Assistance Professional Association UK (EAPA UK)

At the time of writing, the EAPA UK is a small organization that exists as a branch of the North American Employee Assistance Professionals Association (EAPA). In North America, EAPA is a large, successful and well-established organization that has recognition and funding from a large and varied community of support. It experienced some problems regarding membership in 2002 when a large trade union withdrew its activists. However, in North America, the size of the EAP market demands a regulated professional workforce and EAP workers have an accreditation process, which is one of its main assets and differences to EAPs in the United Kingdom. This is the Certified Employee Assistance Professional (CEAP) credential, administered by the Employee Assistance Certification Commission (EACC). To take the CEAP exam an EAP worker has options for eligibility that include 3000 hours of work experience in an EAP setting, 60 professional development hours, a graduate degree in an EAP-related subject and 24 hours of CEAP supervision over six months. The EAP worker has to pay for this process and specific subjects have to be studied and completed. The United Kingdom-based EAPs have very professional EAP workers, but at present only a handful of EAP workers are CEAPs in the UK. In Eire, where there has been an expanding EAP growth, a bold effort to introduce CEAPs has been led by Maurice Quinlan and his training organization.

Most of the EAP workers in the United Kingdom are accredited counsellors and chose this as their primary qualification rather than a CEAP credential. The EAPA UK is trying to establish CEAP as a worthwhile accreditation for British counsellors and EAP workers, but this is a problem as EAPA UK has a small membership and is perceived as 'a providers' club'. Some counsellors refer to the EAPA UK as a trades association that has no interest in counselling and is ineffective because of the fierce economic competition between rival EAPs. The EAPA UK has a different perspective on workplace counselling, as its members are largely drawn from domestic and UK-based EAPs. The EAPA UK is interested in the broad dynamics of organizations, and membership comprises a variety of organizational professionals as well as counsellors.

The EAPA UK produced standards and guidelines documents in 1998, which are currently being updated. These standards have been crucial in defining EAP structures and operations in the United Kingdom. Without these guidelines, there would be very little information to purchasers and providers about what to expect and deliver as an EAP in the United Kingdom. The EAPA UK is looking forward to the growth of workplace counselling for providers and purchasers alike. The differences between the values, positions and perspectives of the ACW and EAPA UK are important, but do not have to prevent cooperation and growth. Both sets of values are essential to workplace counsellors as they reflect the struggles, conflicts and contradictory demands that are faced by those working as counsellors or EAP workers in organizations every day.

CONCLUSION

Tracing the history of workplace counselling is not easy, since it is not well documented. However, reflecting upon individuals such as Freud, Reddy, Jesse Boot, Egan, the Crewcare counsellors, and the recovering alcoholics roaming North America to help fellow employees, is refreshing. It is inspiring and invigorating to imagine the struggles and determination of these people as they doggedly stuck to their ideas and beliefs. Some of the results of their labours are what we know as workplace counselling today.

But what *is* contemporary workplace counselling? I describe this in more detail in Chapter 2.

· TWO ·

The context of workplace counselling

SOME DEFINITIONS

Counselling is so similar to the *listening* that goes on between people and groups of people every day in every workplace, that it is in one sense a very old and common practice. But counselling is not just about listening, it is also a process that provides another person with an opportunity to develop further understanding about himself or herself. So what is counselling in the workplace?

There is a very optimistic tone to Axelrod's recommendations to psychoanalysts on how to begin to provide treatment for patients bringing work-related material to the analysis:

> Drawing on my experience with work-related issues, I have come to believe that there is an irreducible capacity for mature pleasure in work life that is a touchstone of adult development. All forms of work disturbance represent some interference in the satisfaction that *can* be achieved from working. The treatment process is based on intervention to identify the sources of this dissatisfaction and to further the patient's mature pleasure in working. Successful intervention requires the clinician to go beyond pat ideas of success and productivity to address the ways in which working is represented in the patient's mental life. Conflicts and deficits that emerge in the patient's work life are seen in relation to core personality dynamics.
>
> (1999: 78)

He suggests two significant ideas that help develop the notion of what counselling at work actually is. First, people can achieve a mature pleasure in their working lives doing their jobs if they are not interfered with. Second, helping people understand their problems with their work helps them to understand essential elements of their own personality.

The first idea brings to mind a well-known cliché – 'I would be OK if they would just let me get on with my job'. Counsellors in workplaces hear this frequently – employees are constantly complaining about excessive interference from managers, supervisors, colleagues, customers and so on – indeed, anyone who stops the employee doing what they want to do. However, some of those who complain in this way might protest about the suggestion that work is something they want to do – it is not what they *want* to do, but what they *have* to do. We begin to see some of the complicated ways in which we all try to make sense of work – we may not want to do it, but if we have to then we do not want anyone else interfering with what we have to do. The Marxist idea of alienation and the whole question of a person alienated from their true sense of identity by the process of selling their labour has something to be said for it. The possibility that work is an adult's form of play does not sit squarely with a Marxist interpretation.

Axelrod's second important point is the concept of understanding an individual by listening to the material they bring to a therapy session that is directly related to the individual's work. Their ideas, feelings and behaviour relating to work are a reflection of their ideas, feelings and behaviour about their whole life and personality. Alfred Adler (1932: 12) describes the three main problem areas that face us in our lives: occupation, the social and the sexual, and it is 'in his response to these three problems that every individual human being unfailingly reveals his own deep sense of the meaning of life'. The workplace is an aspect of human life that is an essential element in our understanding of ourselves and our worlds. Counselling provided in this environment addresses crucial questions, dilemmas and difficulties about work and helps us develop as humans.

McLeod (2001: 13), in his study of workplace counselling, settles for a definition of counselling as an activity that

> is *voluntarily chosen* by the client . . . *responsive to the individual* . . . an activity that is primarily *intended to bring about change* in an area of psychological/behavioural functioning (e.g. emotional difficulties, relationships, self-esteem, symptoms of depression or anxiety, work functioning, substance misuse, absence from work, etc.).
>
> (McLeod 2001: 13)

Gerard Egan (1993: 7) suggests that counselling is an activity that has value 'only to the degree that it leads to *valued outcomes* in the client's day to day life'. He adds that if 'a helper and client engage in the counselling process effectively, something valued will be in place that was not in place before the helping sessions'.

Egan outlines the four main outcomes from the counselling process: a developed sense of worth and self-confidence, the ability to be more assertive, challenging original patterns of self-defeating behaviour and becoming an agent rather than a patient in everyday life, able to forsake old patterns of being a victim. Egan describes the process of helping as collaboration between client and helper:

> helpers stimulate clients to provide services to themselves. It is the clients who achieve the goals of helping, through the facilitation of the helper. It follows that, while counsellors help clients achieve outcomes, they do not control outcomes. When all is said and done, clients have a greater responsibility for both the production and the quality of outcomes.
>
> (1993: 8)

He uses the word 'helper' interchangeably with counsellor. This is no accident and highlights Egan's anti-elitist view of counselling – many people are able to do it and apply it, and can benefit from the principles of counselling/helping.

The American Counseling Association (ACA) presents its definition of workplace counselling as follows:

> The Practice of Professional Counseling. The application of mental health, psychological or human development principles, through cognitive, affective, behavioural or systemic intervention strategies that address wellness, personal growth, or career development, as well as pathology.
>
> (ACA 2002)

One more definition is useful for the consideration of counselling in the workplace. Colin Feltham (1997: 2) in his introduction to the concepts of 'listening' states:

> Counselling is implicitly about helping people to discover better ways of dealing with personal problems both at home and at work and it is widely recognized that no final distinction can be made between a person's work-based and home-based concerns, since they are inevitably likely to feed into each other.

Counselling is therefore to do with assisting another person with *living*. How is an employee assisted in *living* by talking to a counsellor?

AN EXAMPLE

One example of how a workplace counselling service operates can be seen in the North Staffordshire Combined NHS Healthcare Trust Staff Counselling Service. Established in 1994 the service is available free to approximately 6500 employees of the trust, local primary care trusts and one small local authority. The team currently consists of one manager, who has a small counselling caseload, two counsellors working three days each week and one administrator who is the initial telephone contact for employees accessing the service. The service usually has a student from a local counselling diploma course providing some counselling. All employees self-refer to the service, which is publicized widely through the various worksites. The service covers a large rural area with about 200 different worksites. To meet the geographical challenges of the organization, a satellite office with suitable counselling rooms has been recently established.

The service has a regular slot in every new employee induction programme. It provides courses on stress in the workplace as a means of publicity, and is included in the corporate health and safety training programme for line managers to raise awareness of the service. Flyers and email publicity are also used to ensure employees know how and what the service can offer.

Annual statistics from the service indicate that employees hear about the service through personal recommendation, previous experience and presentation and induction. The counsellor-manager states 'these statistics confirm that the personal contact at inductions/ presentations and word of mouth are still the most effective system of getting information about the service to staff' (North Staffordshire Combined NHS Healthcare Trust 2002). The total number of new clients seen each year is approximately 2 percent of the employee population, with some seasonal variations. Seasonal variations are common in many counselling services – June to September is a quiet period, September to November is busy, there is a quiet time before Christmas and then it is very busy from January onwards. Each employee contacts the service by a telephone call. Occasionally an employee is referred by their line manager after a sickness monitoring interview, but these forms of referral are rare. The service has a first contact protocol, and this is usually the responsibility of the administrator. The administrator asks the employee how much they know about the service and outlines the basic counselling process for them. This includes assessment, the number of sessions employees are entitled to (up to eight sessions), the opportunity to change to another counsellor if the employee wishes to and the possibility of referral to another agency for long-term therapy if appropriate. The emphasis on this initial contact is to try to put the employee at ease – 'to normalize the process' as the administrator puts it and also to check out if counselling is what the employee actually needs. A few other questions are asked of the employee and some of this data is collated for the Client Assessment sheet – (see Appendix I). This early and important part of the workplace counselling process is included on the Service Evaluation Form that each client is given at the end of the process (see Appendix II). Clients are encouraged to comment on this early and important part of contact with the service. The client is sent a confirmation letter for the appointment and a service brochure that outlines some of the boundaries of the service. Most of the counselling takes place in counselling rooms adjacent to the manager's office, which is located in a discreet corridor, sealed off by double doors from other departments, in a small hospital.

The manager provides case management for the counsellors once every two weeks. The case management process is based on the EAPA guidelines and the counsellors are clear about the distinctions between supervision and case management (this is explained in detail in Chapter 4). Each counsellor receives at least one and a half hours of supervision each month from an external supervisor of their choice, which is paid for by the service.

This service is well established in its environment, and has a credible position within the organization. It has to provide a level of self-financing through training programmes, but has adequate financial support from the centre of the organization. The other feature of this internal counselling service is the high level of evaluation, which helps the manager to feed back trends and problems in particular areas to senior management. In this way, the service does not collude with unhealthy practices, managerial styles, bullying and so on, but has a clear and credible voice that is trusted by the employees and management alike.

In that service the rooms are discreetly tucked away. But workplace counselling services are very different and each has its own character, appeal and problems. They can be down dusty, Kafkaesque faded corridors, in the splendour of an old country house or close to the excited buzz of a huge airport where the employees are rushing off to different destinations and where the visitor is almost caught up in their haste.

Most of the counselling rooms are discreet, private and comfortable. There are often some self-help books/manuals in a small bookcase, and the inevitable box of tissues placed tactfully but not too prominently within reach of the client's chair. The size and comfort of the chairs varies, of course. The general wealth of the organization is often reflected in the decor and quality of the counselling room furnishings.

PRESENTING PROBLEMS

Employees use counselling and EAP services for a wide range of problems that vary with each organization. Some are specifically related to the identity and idiosyncrasies of a particular organization. For a comprehensive guide to the sort of problems that may present themselves through an EAP, *The Employee Assistance Treatment Planner* (Oher *et al.* 1998) is a valuable reference point; some examples are (1998: v):

- abusive partner;
- anger management;
- anti-social behaviour;
- anxiety/panic;
- chemical dependence;
- chemical dependence relapse;
- co-worker conflict;
- critical incident;
- depression.

Workplace counselling deals with problems outside work, but those that arise within the work setting are perhaps of particular interest. The NHS service referred to above lists the main areas of work-related presentations as:

- work stress;
- disciplinary matters;
- harassment;
- work relationships;
- depression/anxiety (diagnosed by GP);
- lack of support/resources;
- organizational change;
- complaints;
- violence/aggression.

The NHS example's figures for a recent year show that the majority of work-related problems that employees presented with were work stress, followed by harassment and depression. The figures for work stress and depression had risen from the previous period and this was attributed by the counsellor-manager to employees being more willing to approach their GPs for help with stress.

However, the figures for this service show that the majority of employees attending presented with personal problems. These problems are mainly in the following categories:

- health problems;
- personal relationships;
- bereavement and loss;
- domestic violence/aggression;
- family problems;
- alcohol;
- sexual abuse;
- depression/anxiety (diagnosed by GP).

Personal relationships were the main issue, 'bereavement and loss' was the second highest presenting category.

The counsellor-manager interprets the figures as representing increased awareness of some of the issues in the organization, this being a direct result of the training activities of the internal counselling service who deliver short courses on bereavement and loss and explain how the service counsellors can help employees presenting with these issues. The local trade union also actively promoted an awareness campaign about domestic violence.

INFORMATION SERVICES

There are many more issues that reflect the problems of work and personal lives presented to EAPs. To meet the growing number of presenting problems, and in line with the history of the broad brush approach to helping employees, EAPs often include comprehensive information services as part of their services as well as individual counselling. Information services in British EAPs include up to date and accurate detail for a huge array of everyday problems such as debt and finance, housing, domestic/personal legal issues, employment law and so on. Most of the large EAPs have information departments that use specialists to provide the assistance required by the employees. In the early 1990s, some EAPs (such as ICAS and PPC) started to use the Citizens Advice Bureau (CAB) information systems. These are huge ready-made, accurate, easy to use sources of knowledge, which are easily purchased by the EAPs. As well as buying these systems, EAPs have recruited information specialists from the CAB, local authorities and the voluntary sector. This enables them to use people who are already trained and conversant with the particular skills and knowledge required to provide complex information efficiently to employees.

The information specialists have experienced some interesting differences working for EAPs – usually better rates of pay and conditions and a different client group to work with; for example, helping an employee with debt problems is different to helping an unemployed debt client on a fixed income or state benefits. The emergence of large information systems and specialists has also brought with it new networks for EAPs. One British EAP (ICAS) developed a network of money advisors in the early 1990s that operated along the same lines as a counsellor-affiliate network. Money advisors were recruited to meet the geographical requirements of the customer bases and to provide help for employees with debt/ financial problems, on site, at the employee's home or at an EAP office. As well as providing assistance with debt, the network expanded to include assistance with other financial matters such as investments, stocks/shares, tax, pensions and so on. Whole new markets began to emerge for EAPs that of course brought new problems – in the world of finance, for example, were they selling, helping or both?

There are interesting organizational boundary issues regarding the amount of information that managers decide is appropriate for employees to have through an EAP. For example, some non-unionized companies do not want their employees to have free access to employment law specialists, as this may give the employees too much information that could be used against the company.

INTRODUCTION OF AN EAP TO AN ORGANIZATION

Although increasing numbers of larger institutions have in-house counselling services, there are also a growing number of EAPs who either manage a counselling service within an organization or, just as likely, have a network of counsellors outside the organization. An organization has to 'buy in' to an EAP just as it would buy in any other service it prefers not to run for itself. Most EAPs spend a great deal of time and effort to ensure that the initial 'entry' activities with an organization are carefully managed and that the EAP is promoted to employees correctly. Employees may be invited to attend a formal briefing given by an EAP at the employee's workplace. These briefings can be quite crucial to the take-up of EAP services. Most organizations have a financial interest in the utilization of an EAP. For example, some organizations pay an EAP based on a fixed price for each contact or session. In order to minimize the cost of the EAP, the company may not wish for heavy usage of the service and therefore may be cautious about briefings or any other sessions that may raise the profile of the EAP. Other organizations may pay for the EAP on a 'per capita' arrangement, and therefore it may be very important for them to have maximum use of the EAP to get a return on their investment. With per capita contracts, employee briefings are essential.

At the briefings the employees will be told how to access the external service, hours of availability, services offered, inclusion/exclusion of family members, confidentiality and any other contract details that are relevant to the employees. Some external EAPs offer a range of publicity products to the employees – such as small cards that have all the access details attractively printed on them. Usually there are a variety of leaflets/pamphlets/brochures for employees, clearly and brightly designed, indicating that the EAP company is professional, experienced and available. In some organizations, publicity materials are the only contact or information that an employee may have about an EAP.

An employee accessing an external EAP probably uses a similar route to that of any other counselling service – namely through a telephone conversation with an administrator or an intake consultant. When an employee contacts an EAP, the administrator will take a few rudimentary details to identify the organization the employee belongs to, which will help the administrator determine the services available for the employee. The services available are determined by the contract purchased by the employee's organization. After asking for an outline of the presenting problem the administrator will be able to direct the employee to other relevant EAP staff – such as an information specialist, telephone counsellor, training provider, case manager, critical incident counsellor and so on. Some EAPs have generic administrators who can offer telephone counselling immediately or who refer to specialist information. This is often the case for EAPs that use a call centre where administrators are trained to use a generic script to answer the calls and are all trained to operate to ensure consistency of service to employees. In some EAPs, the recording of data from the client company employee is quite lengthy, but this may be dictated by the organization paying for the EAP. Ethical issues about confidentiality and how much information is returned to the organization can deter some employees from using the service, but again much of this can be influenced by the way in which the EAP is introduced to employees and the position that the organization wants the EAP to occupy for its employees (see Chapter 3 for further discussion of this question).

THE WORK–HOME BALANCE

There is a particular presenting issue that workplace counsellors are continually hearing from many clients – the difficult choices that employees routinely have to make between their working lives and their personal domestic lives. In particular, the choices are about how much time to spend at work, how to fit work around personal arrangements or the other way around, how to fit personal relationships into the few hours an employee may have in the week that are not taken up with work. Some employees have great difficulty trying to be a committed employee and being a parent or partner who is committed to a close relationship. The result can be overwhelming feelings of guilt, anger and depression. Many working men and women experience these difficult moral dilemmas, although more recently the focus in many organizations has been how women 'cope' with the differing demands of work and family life.

Some EAPs provide concierge services for employees who simply do not have the time to undertake the different tasks involved in life outside work, such as shopping, laundry, paying bills and so on. Alienation from everyday life is actively encouraged by many organizations who are keen to maximize the use of their employees. Some employees find this encouragement fulfils some of their own neuroses. Some employees collude with this because of difficulties in personal relationships or family life. Research into workaholism illustrates the blurred boundaries between individual problems and the capacity for organizations to perpetuate these problems in order to meet their own needs.

Workaholism is a common presenting issue in workplace counselling services, however, it is often disguised as a different symptom or issue. This example from a public sector workplace counselling service illustrates how attitudes to self and work can be entangled in other issues. An employee who worked in a busy department contacted the counsellor; initially her presenting issues were about the re-occurrence of minor physical symptoms. As the sessions progressed, the physical symptoms were replaced by complaints about her marriage and after further exploration, both the physical and relationship issues could be attributed, partially, to her attitude to her work and the importance of her work role in her estimation of her self. The counsellor was able to help the employee discuss work in a more open and truthful manner than she had been able to previously. This enabled the employee to confront some difficult internal struggles that had been contributing to a rigid and damaging set of values about work and a 'workaholic' personality. There were other issues about her marriage that she required further assistance with, and was able to find help with from Relate, while her physical symptoms were checked by the occupational health department. But it was the initial discussion about the significance of work that proved an important catalyst for this employee.

The work–life balance issue has been around for some time: since the 1970s when organizations realized they needed to provide childcare services for female employees. Work–life initiatives evolved from work–family principles that had been developing in North America and were closely linked to economic demands. Before industrialization workers had been mainly agricultural and the workplace often was the worker's home. With industrialization many employers provided factories, houses and schools for the workers. However the Depression changed much of this, as did the Second World War. This latter event involved women in mass production on an even greater scale, and organizations adapted to the workforce by providing childcare facilities on-site. Some took responsibility for providing care for employees' children, often on-site. Some childcare centres were reported to be 'open 24 hours a day, 365 days per year to accommodate the round the clock work shifts supporting the war machine' (Davidson and Herlihy 1999).

During the 1950s, women were once again restricted to child rearing in the family home while men were the main earners and so work–family programmes that had been established in organizations were not as popular or necessary. This changed again through the 1960s and into the 1970s when women were returning to the workplace in large numbers. Central government in North America became actively involved in supporting organizations and employees, and by 1982 there were 152 hospital-based childcare centres and 42 industry-based childcare centres (Davidson and Herlihy 1999). However, it was the human resources departments that created employer-based work–family initiatives, and 'subsequently the work–life industry' (Davidson and Herlihy 1999). These departments became important resources for employees and a function known as 'R and R' developed – resource and referral. Inevitably, private companies started to offer these functions and the work–life industry is now an established part of corporate life.

As the demographic profiles and lifestyle of the workforce changed through the 1980s and 1990s, the work–life programmes had to provide more than childcare resources as the *parents* of these workers now required care and so elder-care programmes and referral systems evolved. Elder-care resources are now often included in EAP packages.

Work–life services are different from the clinical activities of workplace counselling as they are not necessarily anything to do with psychological difficulties. Usually the services are involved with finding appropriate child-/elder-care so that the employee can focus on their career and job. In this manner, they are preventative rather than curative (which is how some employers also perceive workplace counselling). Work–life services help employees:

> in finding and selecting quality child care, making decisions regarding adoption, negotiating and communicating with an employee's children's teachers, making vocational or college choices, and orchestrating the necessary resources an employee's older adult parents may require within their communities necessary to maintain normal functioning.
>
> (Davidson and Herlihy 1999: 410)

Work–life services usually focus on helping employees deal with issues and problems that are part of the usual lifecycle. As employees age they are usually faced with a variety of issues that can become problems. There is a parallel process that can flow between life at work, and life outside of work, for example, as a person enters the workplace they may also be embarking on a new stage of a personal relationship; as they get promoted or demoted at work they may leave or start new personal relationships, as they leave one organization and perhaps move to another part of the country to take up new work, they may lose contact with friends and some family members; as they become familiar with their work task and become disappointed sometimes with what they have not achieved, they may be experiencing the physical symptoms of the ageing process. Kets de Vries (1987: 118) suggests that employees go through five stages during their working life that are very similar to ordinary regular life stages for most individuals:

1 reality shock;
2 socialization and growth;
3 mid-career crisis;
4 acceptance;
5 pre-retirement.

As employees engage in these different phases of development, they face differing challenges and struggles that may distract them from their work tasks, or from their personal relationships. Life affects work, work affects life. Home affects work, work affects home. Work–life services recognize the importance of these phases and the interconnectivity between work and home. They offer practical assistance when these important times in life become difficult.

In Europe there has been an increase of women in the workforce. However, many of the jobs they have are part-time and they are still often less well paid than their male equivalents. In the United Kingdom the greatest increase in workforce participation has been among women working with children under 5 years old, from 37 percent in 1984 to 52 percent in 1994. There is a familial and social cost to this increase that many organizations are aware of and attempt to assist their employees with. There is a wide variety of work–life services and provision on offer. Some examples are companies such as Worklife Balance that provide programmes directly to companies and individuals; the Department of Transport and Industry promotes a central government and business initiative; there is the business partnership forum Employers for Worklife Balance; and the Addenbrooke NHS Trust has a work–life policy for their employees. Most of these programmes and policies are concerned with helping employees reduce and manage the working culture of long and unsocial hours, so that they can combine work and family commitments.

Addenbrooke's work–life balance policy, for example, promotes childcare and elder-care, and a range of schemes that include adoption leave, career breaks, parental emergency leave, paternity leave, special leave for IVF treatment and special time-out leave – discretionary unpaid leave up to 12 months for 'eldercare commitments, voluntary work overseas, study or research'. Part-time, self-rostering and bank schemes are also available to employees (Addenbrooke's NHS Trust 2002). The trust's EAP, working hours and jobshare policy thus form part of the work–life balance provision.

INFLUENCES ON COUNSELLING AT WORK

The fundamental theoretical influences on modern counselling that inform and create counselling practice can be grouped under three distinct headings: psychodynamic, person-centred and cognitive-behavioural. What difference do these theories make to the delivery of counselling in the workplace?

McLeod (2001: 4) states that:

There is no evidence that any one approach to counselling is more effective than any other in this field. Positive results have been found using a variety of models of counselling, including cognitive–behavioural, psychodynamic, person-centred, rational emotive and solution focused.

Nevertheless, counsellors are often wedded to the theoretical model in which they were trained. There may be little difference in effectiveness, but there are perhaps differences in how the theories are applied to counselling in the workplace.

THE PSYCHODYNAMIC APPROACH

Psychodynamic counselling is based upon many of the ideas, techniques and principles developed by Sigmund Freud, whose ideas have to some extent become part of everyday language, entering in popular and sometimes misunderstood form into the communication and understanding of many people.

Freud's theory suggests that our personalities are determined at an early age and that much of our early experience stays with us, repressed in the unconscious. Freud also developed a technique, which is still widely used today in psychodynamic counselling, that includes working with transference and counter-transference, recognizing resistances and defences, and interpreting the meaning of the material that the client refers to in the sessions.

By its very nature, the psychodynamic exploration of an individual requires regular sessions, whereby the relationship with the counsellor (including the transference) and the feelings the counsellor has with the client (counter-transference), are explored as possible expressions of how the client relates to others in the past and in the present. This may appear to make the psychodynamic approach difficult to use in the relatively short-term contacts in workplace counselling.

But psychodynamic counselling can be used in workplace settings, with some important modifications. Hood (1995: 248) describes it as the 'challenge . . . to maintain a psychodynamic frame of reference in a setting which is not avowedly therapeutic'. He suggests four features that help a psychodynamic counsellor work in a time-limited setting: the client's expectations; time limits; the context of the client's whole life; and transference. Hood offers between four and eight sessions in his time-limited work focusing on career/vocational issues, and believes it possible to help clients build a worthwhile insight.

One example of an internal EAP providing psychodynamic counselling is the service in a local authority of approximately 18,000 employees. Other forms of counselling are also provided, but psychodynamic counselling is offered to a small number of employees whose problems combine work and personal issues, and who, although still functioning, may present as being 'quite disturbed'. The manager has a multi-purpose role that includes a small psychodynamic caseload. The manager selects employees who are suitable for brief psychodynamic counselling of one session a week for up to 12 sessions or, for some clients, on-going psychodynamic counselling.

Martha, for instance, was referred to the internal EAP by a personnel officer, because her line manager had complained about her aggression and of occasions in the office when she had 'snapped'. The personnel officer telephoned the EAP manager and asked if this was an appropriate issue for the EAP, and how she might suggest to Martha that it would be a good idea for her to contact the counsellors. The EAP manager provided some information about referral and briefed the personnel officer on how to recommend the EAP services without threatening or coercing the employee.

A few days later, Martha contacted the EAP and an assessment appointment was arranged. The assessment session identified some key areas for the work and assessed her suitability for time-limited psychodynamic counselling. Suitability was decided on psychological mindedness, in other words, 'a capacity for self-observation or self-appraisal as opposed to rationalization' (Cooper and Alfille 1998); recent onset of problems; evidence of external support; ability to use the transference and a trial interpretation; and (for the counsellor) a therapeutic plan.

The counsellor and employee contracted to work together for 12 weekly sessions, at the same time and venue. The focus of the work was Martha's anger and how this affected her working life. This focus came from Martha herself. Martha wanted to discuss her anger at work and to try to understand its causes. The counsellor discussed with Martha the possibilities of doing this within a short period of time, and that such exploration may only be a beginning for Martha. In his supervision the counsellor said that he felt that he was slightly concerned about containing some of Martha's anger in a short counselling contract, and that some of the anger that he sensed coming from her in the counselling room would probably require a much longer exploration. The counsellor noted some positive transference initially – but that it was almost *too* positive. During an early session, the counsellor felt that the positive transference was changing into some form of idealization that might reveal something about Martha's early relationships, and how these were unconsciously repeated in the workplace. However, the brevity of the sessions prevented this theory from being confirmed – although a simple link was made during one of the later sessions.

After the 12 sessions Martha reported positively that the counselling had helped: she had expressed much that she felt had not been expressed before, and she was able to recognize some of her early struggles being repeated in some of her relationships at work. One of the themes touched upon in the sessions was the re-occurrence of Martha being ignored, neglected and left on her own by a significant authority figure: first in her early life by her mother and later in her working life by her female line manager.

This example serves as a useful reminder of the complexity and multiple layers of meaning and projection of some problems that psychodynamic counsellors have to deal with in short-term counselling contracts. Twelve sessions were helpful but more could have been done if the counsellor had been able to offer more sessions. Further work might have led to a deeper understanding of some of the issues around being neglected as a small child and how this had reappeared in the employee's experiences in the workplace.

Offering the possibility of psychodynamic work in this service meant assessing those who could benefit from short-term interventions and those who were suitable for medium-term psychodynamic work (although the length of medium-term varies from writer to writer on brief work). A small number of employees received once weekly sessions for up to two years. But the debate about the length of psychodynamic work in workplace settings has not been fully addressed, especially since the main determinant of the number of sessions has been an economic rather than a clinical decision. The provision of medium- and long-term counselling in the workplace is one that requires further exploration in British organizations.

The humanistic approach

Humanistic counselling and therapy is widely used in workplace counselling. The term covers a wide range of theories and practices, but one of the major contributors to theory and practice is Carl Rogers, who described key values that are important in the counsellor such as belief in the 'significance and worth of each person'

(Rogers 1951: 21) and three core conditions that must be present to promote growth in the individual: 'genuineness, realness or congruence', 'unconditional positive regard' and 'empathic understanding' (1980: 115–16). A major feature of his theory is the notion of the actualizing tendency as a natural feature of all living organisms, which Rogers describes as: 'in every organism, at whatever level, an underlying flow of movement toward constructive fulfilment of its inherent possibilities. In humans beings, too, there is a natural tendency toward a more complex and complete development' (1980: 117).

An example of humanistic counselling in the workplace can be seen in the service offered to British Airways employees. Chris is a person-centred counsellor who works for Crewcare, the British Airways internal 'peer' counselling service. Trained and experienced as a cabin crew member, he has been working at Crewcare since 1994 for six days each month. This includes working in the Crewcare office and providing night cover from home.

The initial training that Chris received as part of the selection and recruitment of the Crewcare team used the Egan Three Stage Skilled Helper model (Egan 2002). The model is essentially humanistic as the goal of the helping is always towards 'client-enhancing outcomes'. After this, Chris then undertook a person-centred training. He feels strongly about the person-centred approach but admits that he did have difficulty in making the adjustments from his private practice to the time-limited, structured and staged way of using the Egan model in the workplace. However, with the help of experienced workplace counselling supervision he has been able to integrate the person-centred training with the Egan model. He is also very aware of the tension that exists between trying to help the client move on in the Egan model, and the person-centred way of trying to go at the client's pace without leaving the client feeling more vulnerable and unsupported.

An important feature of person-centred counselling is the counsellor's use of self, in particular self-disclosure. Chris believes that sometimes it is useful for him to use personal disclosure because Crewcare is fundamentally a 'peer support' service. In this setting all the clients are aware that the counsellors are serving cabin crew and may have similar cabin crew experiences. This is one of the main features and successful attributes of Crewcare.

He has had to find a workable compromise between his core person-centred theoretical training and the requirements of this particular counselling service. The 'one-off' nature of crisis sessions Chris has with cabin crew may be a reflection of their transitory working lives – here today, somewhere else tomorrow – and of the temporary relationships aircrew have with passengers on any flight. The concept of a 'peer' service can be closely linked to some of Rogers' ideas about empathy – 'I understand what this feels like when I have been there, it may be similar to how you feel' or 'I know what it is like for me to do this job'. Chris recognizes that this important combination of empathy and experience make the service appropriate and successful for the employee population.

The cognitive-behavioural approach

The third main approach to workplace counselling is cognitive-behavioural counselling or cognitive-behavioural therapy (CBT). McLeod (2001: 79) refers to a survey to examine brief counselling used by EAP counsellors. It concluded that while most of the EAP counsellors were originally trained as psychodynamic or person-centred practitioners, most reported using cognitive-behavioural techniques in EAP work. Perhaps one of the reasons is the ease in adapting some of the more directive and educational processes that comprise the cognitive-behavioural approach to the time limit of brief counselling.

The principles of CBT include the influence of negative thinking patterns upon individual's feelings and behaviours. By recognizing negative thoughts, they can then be challenged and compared to reality. Replacing critical, unhelpful and damning negative thoughts about events and situations can lead to more effective ways of behaving, living and experiencing according to two major influences on CBT: Albert Ellis and Aaron Beck.

An example of the successful application of CBT is evident from the approach used by a large external EAP provider. A company approached the EAP about one of their employees who had been downloading pornography from the Internet while at work. He was a key member of staff, so that while the behaviour constituted gross misconduct, which usually would result in instant dismissal, the company did not want to lose him. They asked the EAP if there was any help he could have that would assist him in changing his behaviour. The EAP arranged for a counsellor to do an assessment to determine if the employee was suitable for a CBT approach. The assessment revealed that the employee exhibited the characteristics of 'addictive personality' and certain addictive behaviour patterns. The employee had ten sessions with the CBT counsellor and the focus of the sessions was to change the addictive behaviour that threatened his work for his company, rather than try to change the addictive personality. The counselling was successful; he stopped his problematic behaviour and continued to work well for the company.

Crisis counselling

Many employee counselling services and EAPs include some form of 'crisis counselling'. 'Crisis counselling' is a generic term incorporating the functions of debriefing and counselling for post-traumatic stress disorder (PTSD). Scott and Stradling (1998) quote an estimated figure of 1 percent of the population at any one time being affected by PTSD. The revised DSM definition contains the following five criteria:

1 The client must have witnessed or experienced a serious threat to their life or physical well-being.
2 The client must re-experience the event in some way.
3 The client must persistently avoid stimuli associated with the trauma or experience a numbing of general responsiveness.
4 The client must experience persistent symptoms of increased arousal.
5 Symptoms must have lasted at least a month.
        (DSM Criteria-111-R, cited in Scott and Stradling 1998)

During the First World War, some psychiatrists began to listen to the stories of their patients who had experienced the horrors of military action; indeed psychoanalysis became more widespread because of its early use in this way. During the Second World War soldiers were treated in groups, leading to the development of group therapy; additionally in North America groups of soldiers were given debriefing sessions, which helped them to communicate in a slightly different manner and aided recovery. This method spread to the emergency services as a basic model for debriefing.

Currently there is a debate surrounding the practices of debriefing, as outlined by Galliano (2002: 20). Some critics have suggested, following some research, that debriefing is damaging. However, Galliano asserted that Critical Incident Processing and Recovery (CIPR) intervention can be useful for clients if used sensitively and objectively. This debate seems to be an old one applied to counselling as a whole – does it work or does it cause more harm? Critical incident counselling is still in its infancy in the United Kingdom. However, it is a service most counselling organizations believe they should provide.

Particular companies look for the provision of a critical incident service – for example, banks and building societies, whose employees are frequently subject to robberies, violence and other forms of trauma. A behavioural definition of critical incident includes:

1 Experienced or witnessed a traumatic event which involved actual or threatened death, serious injury or threat to physical integrity.
2 Repeated flashbacks or persistent, unwanted memories of the traumatic event that make concentration difficult and heighten feelings of anxiety or depression.
3 Sleep difficulties and/or appetite disturbances following the traumatic event.
4 Significant apprehension and/or fear of a repeat of the traumatic incident that make it difficult to carry out job responsibilities.
5 Feeling emotionally numb and having difficulty finding pleasure or happiness in usual life tasks following the traumatic event.
6 Heightened post-trauma irritability and anger.
7 Stress-related post-trauma psycho-physiological problems such as low back pain, headaches and gastrointestinal disorders.

(Oher *et al.* 1998: 47)

There are many examples of employees who have received help after events such as plane crashes, rail disasters, terrorist incidents, bank robberies, road traffic accidents, the suicide of other employees and sudden death of family members.

Independent Counselling and Advisory Services (ICAS) has a specific crisis model that outlines what can be provided by counsellors specializing in this form of intervention. The Critical Incident Processing and Recovery model (CIPR) consists of five phases which help employees describe what happened to them, or what they witnessed, chronologically, 'from a place of safety, to a place of safety'. The phases include analysis of facts, thoughts and reactions after the incident, normalization and coping and closure. The process is directive, helping employees focus on recovery in a safe and well-contained environment. It is often provided for groups of employees, but it is not the intention of the crisis counsellors to uncover intense emotional reactions. If these do arise, they are swiftly and sensitively contained. Appropriate individual help is provided, but in a group situation the intention is not to re-traumatize employees. The crisis counsellors contain emotional reactions and keep employees in a 'cognitive domain'. Part of the ICAS service includes the assessment of the needs of an organization conducted by critical incident managers who provide a briefing for the crisis counsellors called in to provide CIPR either on-site, or at a convenient location for the employees.

CONCLUSION

In this chapter I have described what counselling in the workplace is, and some of the issues that are brought to counsellors in that setting. In the last part of the chapter I have outlined some of the theories used in counselling in the workplace, and the influence the setting has upon their delivery.

It is a major decision for an organization to ask a counsellor or an EAP to look after the psychological health of their employees. Many organizations do not know much about counselling theory, nor do they have to. It is counsellors who need to know what it is in their theory and practice that is most applicable to the workplace. As yet, there is no single 'workplace counselling theory', although there is a growing amount of experience and practice to explore. It may indeed be that the different theoretical models all have something to offer. One approach may help a particular client more than another.

The problems that employees bring to workplace counselling are similar to those in any other counselling setting, although there are some important issues about life and work that employees bring *because* the counselling service is at work, or is offered to them by their employer. The impact of work upon life and of home upon work is a key issue for workplace counsellors. Sometimes it is heavily disguised in other symptoms or issues, but it is a constant. And if issues about work are the 'bedrock' of counselling in this context, so too are issues about working in this context vital to the counsellor. It is to these that I turn in Chapter 3.

· THREE ·

The practice of counselling at work

There are three major areas that affect all counsellors in the work setting and in the organization for which they are working. Each of the areas reflects upon their position within the organization:

- How will confidentiality of the counselling relationships be maintained?
- How much will the counselling role be limited to counselling or expanded into other functions?
- How will the organization decide on the value of counselling, that is, the effectiveness of the counselling provided, and the manner in which this is measured, perceived and used by the organization and counselling service?

These three issues are fundamental boundaries that help (or hinder) the establishment and maintenance of the counsellor's position in the workplace.

Questions about confidentiality, dual relationships and evaluation also assist in demarcating where counselling begins and ends for an organization, and may help the counsellor to comprehend where he or she belongs in it and in its day to day life. The answers to these questions may also show whether or not he or she is important to the organization.

Before exploring the nature of these three major areas, it is useful to consider the process whereby an organization decides that it needs to offer counselling. This is because the early interest in counselling and the perceived need for it in a company or public body establishes important values that impact on confidentiality, the recognition and possibility of dual relationships and expectations about evaluation of counselling.

Why does an organization want to invite in a counsellor or team of counsellors to listen to employees? What does it hope to gain from such activity? Who proposes this activity and how do they go about establishing that their employees need it? Who tells them that their employees will benefit from counselling? Is counselling perceived as a benefit for employees? In other words, who is the counselling for? These are complex questions that need to be asked in order to understand this particular context. Counselling in the workplace may appear to be a random service provided to employees that has accidental evolutionary origins in the organization. It may have rather unremarkable origins or even unknown origins. One large multinational company, for example, when asked about their counselling services, was unable to identify precisely where, when or why the service developed.

It is often a manager or personnel manager who decides that counselling may be useful. It is rarely the employees as a unified group who decide they want it – usually someone makes a decision on behalf of the majority of the workforce. How often are the employees involved in the decision to bring in a counsellor? And if they are, do those individuals actually use the service? Is it for them or for everyone else? Are these employees unconsciously acting for the others? It is rather like a parent deciding their children need therapy, but the parent not taking part in the therapy. Sometimes it may be appropriate for the parent to be part of the therapy, sometimes not; but sometimes they abdicate their responsibility by arranging the therapy for their children.

It is possible that an organization brings in a counsellor, only to hear what cannot be heard, or to hear what it does not want or need to hear. For example, an employee struggling with a difficult relationship with a line manager may present issues that the organization does not want to hear about – in many places of work the relationships between line manager and employee are often completely ignored. The problems that an employee has with his or her family may be something that an organization also decides it does not need to hear.

A counsellor also has to be chosen. BACP offers some basic guidelines on what to look for in selecting a counsellor, and the EAPA provides a booklet outlining the process a company or institution might go through to select an EAP provider. Apart from this, there is little information to assist a personnel manager or the occupational health team in working out how to select a counsellor. Yet this is an important task, inviting in an individual, or team of individuals, just as it would be to invite a therapist into a family – the counsellor may hear all sorts of stories and complaints about abuses within the organization, about managers, colleagues, policies and so on. Selection has to be very carefully considered, so that the person who is chosen is sensitive to the concerns and fears that some people may have. Some may feel threatened by the presence of a counsellor in the organization; some will worry that the arrival of the counsellor indicates a level of mental distress – in fact, many different fantasies are projected onto the counsellor long before they arrive.

Some employers give serious thought to these matters, but there is still a high degree of misunderstanding about the nature and function of counselling in the workplace, not just by employers, but also among employees and counsellors. This leads to counsellors working in unsuitable settings – and while sometimes this is recognized, often it is not. Many counsellors are chosen for their skills, abilities and personality traits, which personnel and other non-counselling managers readily identify, and they provide an excellent service. But some are chosen on the basis of non-counselling criteria. Counsellors often occupy complex positions in organizations. How they respond to the intricate projections that can be made will depend on their training and personality and how the organization facilitates them. This in turn depends on many internal factors within the institution.

Lack of clear information about the training, skills and functions of workplace counsellors requires the people doing the recruiting to rely on their own training and perceptions – and they are usually from non-counselling backgrounds. Thus, counsellors may not be recruited for their paperwork counselling credentials, and this leads to organizations getting the counsellors they deserve. It is the same as when an individual chooses a counsellor or therapist – the choice is made on the basis of a whole range of conscious and unconscious factors, all of which may be relevant to the future of the relationship between client and counsellor.

When personnel managers recruit counsellors, they have to think about how the employees will respond to the person they appoint. Is the counsellor the appropriate gender, race, age and class to fit the setting? But then, does the counsellor have to 'fit in'? If the service is seen as separate or independent of the organization, is the counsellor chosen as someone who will look different or separate? Is the selection made on the basis of a stereotype of what counselling is? What position is the counsellor expected to occupy in the structure, and how does this determine selection? What boundaries, parameters, contracts, tasks, functions, operations, results, feedback, outcomes or relationships are expected from and projected onto the counsellor from the beginning? How are all these complex issues assessed in the initial selection of the counsellor? Most of these issues for the majority of organizations and counsellors are not even recognized.

As a simple guideline to those establishing a counselling service, the following questions may be useful when considering a particular counsellor or service provider:

1 What is a counsellor/ counselling service needed for?
2 What level of counselling training is appropriate for those needs?
3 What will the counsellor need to understand about their role?
4 What do they have discretion to do, over and above their counselling?
5 How might employees perceive the counsellor?
6 Where will the counsellor/counselling service be situated? And what does this site say about the place of counselling in the organization?
7 Does the counsellor need to 'fit into' or, if necessary, 'fit outside of' the organization?

WHY HAVE A COUNSELLING SERVICE?

Organizations appear to believe that their employees will benefit from counselling. But why?

First, because counselling providers, EAPs and individual counsellors who market their services suggest that they will be good for the organization and that employees will benefit; that production will increase; that absence will be reduced; that harassment and claims will be reduced; and that psychological well-being will be improved generally. This has indeed been documented and supported by many sources, including John McLeod's (2001) research.

Second, a Court of Appeal (5 February 2002) decision has helped to promote counselling services. Three cases of psychiatric injury caused by work-related stress were overturned by Lord Justice Brooke, Lady Justice Hale and Lord Justice Kay for a variety of reasons. One of the reasons was that: 'An employer who offers a confidential advice service, with referral to appropriate counselling or treatment services, is unlikely to be found in breach of duty of care' (Court of Appeal 2002).

The judges made some interesting observations that show insight into services that can be provided for employees by an employer:

The key is to offer help on a completely confidential basis. The employee can then be encouraged to recognise the signs and

seek that help without fearing its effects upon his job or prospects; the employer need not make intrusive inquiries or over-
react to such problems as he does detect; responsibility for
accessing the service can be left with the people who are best
equipped to know what the problems are, the employee, his
family and friends; and if reasonable help is offered either directly or through referral to other services, then all that reasonably could be done has been done. Obviously, not all employers
have the resources to put such systems in place, but an employer
who does have a system along these lines is unlikely to be found
in breach of his [sic] duty of care towards his employees.

(Court of Appeal 2002)

One conclusion from this is that it is unlikely that an organization
can be sued for work-related stress if they provide a confidential
counselling service for their employees. The courts are now supporting and endorsing workplace counselling. How this will be used by
organizations that do not have counselling services will have to be
seen. There were different responses to this decision, ranging from
relief by some employers for clarity in what has been a very vague
and difficult issue to prove, through to distrust and cynicism by some
trade union officials regarding a decision that appears to support a
firmer definition of stress, and which has previously been defined
almost entirely by individual subjective experience.

There is therefore an additional motive to having a counselling
service – it will protect employers against employee claims of work-
related stress. Previously some of these claims have been financially
significant – up to £250,000, for example. Perhaps this will lead to
some organizations contracting with a counselling service simply so
that they can say that they have such a service, although what the
implications will then be for the quality and function of that service
will need monitoring. This would be an extension of the 'insurance'
concept of workplace counselling that has existed in some quarters.

The Association of Counselling at Work (ACW) had some concerns
about the Court of Appeal's ruling, which were expressed by the then
chair in the ACW journal:

Is counselling going to become a last defence against litigation? As
an employer, then, I am going to want to know a lot more about
what goes on in that service. I may want to know who is using the
service, and for what reason. Is there a corresponding danger
that disgruntled employees may see opportunities for using
counselling as a weapon in their fight against their employer?

(McInnes 2002)

These are important questions, although not all employers are interested in the detail of the counselling service they pay for, even after this ruling. But the ruling and the response by employers to the ruling relate to the manifold projections that workplace counsellors experience. Often the counsellor or the counselling service can become a symbol of either the employer or of the complaints of the employees. However, the ruling is an interesting one for the ACW, for workplace counsellors and for employees' representatives, as it adds to the debate and may be useful for future definitions of work-related stress.

What other workplace injuries justify the establishment of a counselling service? Hirshhorn describes 'normal psychological injuries' as 'the normal, expectable hurts that people experience as they try to collaborate with others in implementing an organization's primary tasks within an uncertain environment' (2000: 26). In other words, working with other people to achieve a common goal involves ordinary conflict and injury. The nature of relationships within organizations reflects some of the anxieties about the world outside. In order to feel that individuals have some form of control over their lives, they may try to establish control over others; and of course nearly every work setting has to have some structure of authority and control which can either work well or become the focus for the acting out of personal control issues. Individual internal struggles are reproduced in all the groups that we belong to in our lives. Work produces anxiety, and some of this anxiety is normal. Hirschorn (2000) provides examples of how people feel discounted, unappreciated, persecuted, frustrated and manipulated, as a work group tries to achieve its tasks against the background of many forms of external control.

BOUNDARY ISSUES

Boundaries are seen by counsellors as being an essential element of the counselling relationship with clients. However, there is scant definition of the term in the British Association for Counselling and Psychotherapy or in the American Counseling Association's Codes of Ethics and Practice. This may be because there are different theoretical interpretations and applications of boundaries according to the particular counselling model which is being followed.

The term 'boundary' is borrowed from group analysis and may be given other names, as Molnos (1995: 32) identifies. Most of the different terms mean the same thing: 'the special space that in the therapeutic situation is established and maintained by the therapist through the boundaries' (Molnos 1995: 26). Molnos outlines four main categories of boundaries: place, time, conduct and relationship. These are particularly useful for the context of workplace counselling as all of them relate to the three main points explored in this chapter: place relates to confidentiality; time is one aspect of evaluation; and conduct and relationship can be applied to questions related to dual relationships. Molnos's examples of boundaries of place include two common difficulties faced by some workplace counsellors – availability of suitable rooms and external noise. These problems have an impact upon the counselling process and relationship, and workplace counsellors who have difficulties in these areas need to address the boundary disturbances with the employee, and perhaps with the organization itself.

Gray describes the elements that constitute the frame in which the therapeutic process occurs:

> a private setting in which therapist and client meet; fixed times and duration for the sessions; vacation breaks which are clearly stated by the therapist; a set fee for all sessions reserved; and an internal concept on the part of the therapist that what is talked about is not talked about with anyone else outside the therapeutic relationship.
>
> (1994: 7)

There are many other useful descriptions of the therapeutic frame which add depth to the concept, in particular in Langs (1998) and Malan (2001). The main emphasis is on the therapist to try to ensure that the right conditions are 'regulated' (Freud [1913] 2001: 355) in order for the therapy/counselling to begin. It is the counsellor's responsibility to ensure basic boundaries are in place and acknowledged. But in the context of workplace counselling many of these issues are far less clear. There is, for example, no fee (but neither is there in many other settings, such as in education or primary care). Privacy is far less easy to ensure. Fixed times can be difficult, particularly for those working on shifts. And confidentiality is a particular issue.

CONFIDENTIALITY

Confidentiality assumes almost a sacred quality for the vast majority of counsellors, but it can be difficult to apply all the nuances of the values and conventions of private practice counselling in workplace settings. Counsellors in the workplace try to abide by the BACP

Ethical Framework (2002), but on an everyday basis some of them
have to use a code which is part of the employing organization as
well. The BACP code and an organization's code may be very
different.

Counsellors are (in the Oxford Dictionary's definition of confidentiality) 'entrusted with secrets', and being trustworthy is a crucial quality that a counsellor has to establish quickly with a client in
order for the process to begin. As Bond (2000) suggests, confidentiality is more than keeping secrets, it is 'fundamental to the trust and
integrity of the counselling relationship'. However, there are some
secrets that a counsellor cannot keep to himself or herself and may
have to divulge to another party or agency, with the consent of the
client. Knowing how and when this is necessary relies upon the
personal judgement of the counsellor, combined with good training,
experience and clear boundaries informed by professional
standards.

Confidentiality is a counsellor's tool. It is an essential concept that
has to be identified, communicated to and understood by each client.
It is one of the key elements in counselling, forming the background
to the necessary personal attributes and skills such as accurate
listening, patience, clarity of understanding, objectivity and
sensitivity.

There are agreed principles about confidentiality among counsellors that are written into formal statements of practice and established in the professional organization's codes of practice. For
example, BACP and the American Counseling Association (ACA)
incorporate specific sections about it in their codes. In a recent BACP
statement it is found under the heading 'Keeping trust':

> Respecting client confidentiality is a fundamental requirement
> for keeping trust. The professional management of confidential-
> ity concerns the protection of personally identifiable and sensi-
> tive information from unauthorised disclosure. Disclosure may
> be authorised by client consent or the law. Any disclosures
> should be undertaken in ways that best protect the client's trust.
> Practitioners should be willing to be accountable to their clients
> and to their profession for their management of confidentiality
> in general and particularly for any disclosures made without
> their client's consent.
>
> (BACP 2002: para. 16)

In the section of the ACA *Code of Ethics and Practice* regarding
confidentiality there is the following paragraph about exceptions:

The general requirement that counsellors keep information confidential does not apply when disclosure is required to prevent clear and imminent danger to the client or others or when legal requirements demand that confidential information be revealed. Counselors consult with other professionals when in doubt as to the validity of an exception.

(ACA 1995)

If a situation arises whereby a counsellor needs to breach the agreed confidentiality boundary then the counsellor needs to obtain consent from the client. Consent is best understood if it is written, suggests Darick (1999), in the context of workplace counselling, and she recommends the following five items are included (1999: 9):

1 The person or agency to which the information will be disclosed.
2 The address of the person or agency.
3 The purpose of the disclosure of the information.
4 The date signed.
5 The length of time the consent to disclose is valid and a secondary disclosure clause that is a prohibition against redisclosure without client consent.

Confidentiality, real and perceived, is a major factor for the success of an EAP. Darick offers guidance on how referrals from managers/other employees can be dealt with sensitively and discreetly by an EAP counsellor:

Generally, the supervisor making the referral or the employer can disclose any information about a referred employee to the EAP; however, the EAP can only provide information about a referred employer or supervisor in accordance with the policies and procedures of the program, the conditions of the Statement of Understanding, and the client's signed consent form.

(Darick 1999: 10)

Later she states that 'an EAP clinician should not confirm knowledge of an employee's attendance in EAP without signed release of information or as a result of the aforementioned mandatory disclosure exceptions mentioned' (1999: 10).

These guidelines give an impression of a thorough and rigorous approach to confidentiality that has evolved as a necessity, as well as reflecting ideological principles of respect and care for the client. The principles are clear. The application and pressures upon confidentiality are tested in every setting and probably by every client in different ways. But in a workplace counselling service it is not just determined by the counsellors. The counsellors will hopefully influence the manner in which confidentiality is understood and accepted by individual employees who use the service, but the concept has also to be understood in the context of the employing organization.

Some organizational uses of the term conflict greatly with the counselling understanding of the concept. For example, in a social services department in a local authority, social workers have a variety of semantic options for 'confidentiality'. Confidentiality in some contexts can simply mean a social worker may not discuss a service user's issue with another service user, but the matter can be widely discussed within the office regardless of consent or other principles. A workplace counsellor in a local authority setting needs to be aware of what they may be implying or suggesting when they use the term with clients from such a department. They need to understand the application and interpretation of the term in that particular environment.

In an article in the *Counselling and Psychotherapy Journal*, Jenkins indicates that the promise of absolute confidentiality is no longer possible, and is probably impossible anyway as a counsellor has to discuss a client in supervision, whether or not the client's real name or a pseudonym is used. He states: 'Crucially, the potential restrictions on confidentiality will depend on the context in which the counsellor works' (Jenkins 2002). He outlines the basic legal outlines of confidentiality, the obligations a counsellor has regarding the contract with a client and with the organization funding the counselling, and the sensitive judgements a counsellor may choose to make based upon the 'greater good of society' (Jenkins 2002). A promise of confidentiality is no longer a cast iron guarantee that a counsellor can give either to a client, or to an organization. Jenkins concludes:

> The courts and police can each obtain access to counselling records via specific authority. Not least, the client (or perhaps former client, in some cases) can obtain access to counselling records under data protection law. Counsellors therefore need to be cautious about offering a promise of confidentiality to clients which they may be increasingly unlikely to afford in practice.
>
> (Jenkins 2002)

In North America, Oher (1999) reminds us, there are many other constraints on the confidential relationship between employee and EAP. One of these constraints is the legal obligation regarding positive drug/alcohol tests. Department of Transport records about an employee's drug/alcohol tests are usually confidential, but must be disclosed to those employees within an organization who are responsible for implementation of drug-free workplace programmes. These employees may well be substance abuse professionals (SAPS) involved with an EAP or working directly for an EAP. While they are not counsellors, the onus on these professionals is a reminder of the complexity of confidentiality in the workplace.

Reddy (1998) identifies the reluctance of some employees to use workplace counselling services because of their uncertainty about how personal information, if it is not confidential, may prejudice their future with an organization. He also recognizes how some managers feel uncomfortable with employees revealing personal information to them: 'Quite reasonably they may be afraid of having their hands tied wittingly or unwittingly, by an employee's openness about a personal problem' (1998: 131).

This anxiety reflects an underlying theme in many workplaces: that 'work is not a personal place – there is no place here for personal problems'. This may never be spoken, but it is a common belief that supports the Marxist idea that when a person becomes an employee they become alienated from aspects of their personality. The issue of confidentiality highlights this problem very finely.

Carroll and Walton (1997) point out that principles regarding confidentiality in the counselling world have been quite well established, and individuals are continuing to analyse and add to the canon of counselling ethics surrounding confidentiality. The main issue for workplace counsellors is gaining consent from clients to breach any confidentiality agreement openly entered into at the beginning of the counselling process.

Another way of thinking about the issue is to understand how secrecy is inevitably part of the life of an organization. The counsellor's confidentiality creates quite deliberately, for honourable reasons, a secret relationship. In family terms, a secret relationship is formed, that is not shared outside of the relationship, no matter how hard other family members try to find out, or find access to the relationship or material that binds two of them together. This may create competition, envy and jealousy within a family group because one family member has a relationship that the others do not have. This form of competition or envy can also be reproduced within organizations. One way of defending against these anxieties is to deny the importance of such a relationship or to denigrate the individual who has such a relationship as being weak, unprofessional, unable to cope, mentally unstable and so on. In a family this sort of relationship may be seen as favouritism, granting of special privileges or an unhealthy closeness between two family members. This is something else that workplace counsellors need to recognize – their services will be the target for many projections, including a complex split between unconscious envy and conscious resistance in the form of devaluing the need for the service.

Many organizational defences can therefore be evident in the counselling room, shown in the individual behaviour and perceptions of the counsellor, and in the defensiveness of the employee. Conscious resistance will have many manifestations from the top to the bottom of the organizational hierarchy. The way the service was introduced will tell the prospective counsellor much about the fantasies and anxieties that surround what the service will provide.

A different perspective is taken on this issue by Egan, who does not usually discuss confidentiality when he is listening to employees. He suggests that the burden of confidentiality should not be put upon the counsellor, and the counsellor should be able to enter into an organization with rules about confidentiality already known by the employees. Egan starts his work with employees with a basic premise – 'do no harm'. But he has asked himself many times: 'do no harm, but to whom?' Since the work takes place in a specific environment, and not in a vacuum, he is bound by legal obligations that pertain to the environment. He has a contract with the organization that specifies his function. So that 'do no harm' applies to the organization as well as to individual employees. Egan makes it quite clear what his function has been in many companies: 'if counselling helps, ok. If not, then you're gone. Overt behaviour is the procreation of counselling in an organization. Confidentiality is irrelevant'. What Egan usually says to an employee (in his work these employees are usually senior managers) at the beginning of their discussion is this: 'Both of us are paid by this organization, and you might benefit from our discussion'.

Egan believes that some of the problems employees and counsellors have in the workplace regarding confidentiality are due to Western cultural norms that focus on the rights of the individual rather than on the needs of the group. This raises one of the paradoxes of workplace counselling – helping an individual takes place in a specific group context. Of course, this is true of other forms of counselling where an individual may also be part of a family and/or in a personal relationship with another person. Rarely does an individual have no other human connection. But the workplace is different. All individuals in the organization share a common task, to a greater or lesser degree, and are bound together by association with a mutual interest in that organization's operation and function. Even if colleagues hate each other, through their tasks and the organization, they are mutually bound to each other, and a workplace counsellor becomes part of this dynamic. To ignore the wider group is unwise.

Examples of breaches of confidentiality are usually found in the problems surrounding entry into a workplace counselling service and 'other interested parties'. The entry issue concerns the real physical setting of a counselling service. At one service employee-clients have to go through a main reception area to meet the counsellor. The company is very security-conscious and no employee or visitor can enter the building without signing in a 'visitors' book' and obtaining a swipe card from the reception staff. Unfortunately, some of the reception staff do not realize that employee-clients are not obliged to 'sign in the book'. This means that reception staff may take details of employee-clients who are going to see the counsellor and record the name, department, date and time of the visit, car registration number and so on. It was some time before an employee complained to the counsellor and then the counsellor was able to prevent it happening again, but many employee-clients had already been through this exposing process, whereby anyone in the company who wanted to know who was seeing the counsellor only had to look in the 'visitors' book'. Also, unfortunately, the behaviour of the reception staff in this busy public thoroughfare added to the humiliation of the employee-clients. This is an example of how easily confidentiality can be completely destroyed and how difficult it can be for an employee to access a service. It is also quite a common problem and shows how location has a direct impact upon confidentiality.

Many workplace counsellors are asked by 'interested parties' if an employee has contacted them or been to see them. Often the 'interested parties' are managers who may have referred or encouraged an employee to attend a counselling service. Usually they are concerned about the well-being of an employee or sometimes about their own relationship with an employee, and this prompts them to ask the question. Fellow employees may also have an interest in an employee seeking counselling. For example, human resources officers may have legal reason for referring an employee for counselling. In one local authority, a counsellor received a letter from the human resources department requesting details about the date and time that an employee contacted the counselling service, and for details of the counselling that had been offered to the employee. The employee was threatening to take the authority to court for failing to provide help when they requested it. The counsellor replied politely and firmly that she was unable to disclose such information without written consent from the employee, and that all employees had access to the service. This counsellor knew that it was important to be clear and polite about the issue and that she had to maintain a good relationship with the human resources department as well as to respect and preserve the fundamental ethical boundaries of employee-client confidentiality. A further informal discussion took place and the counsellor offered to meet with a group of new employees in the human resources department to explain the code of ethics that the counsellor was adhering to, and that it was not that she was 'being awkward'. Counsellors in this setting often find 'interested parties' trying to breach these boundaries in many different ways, often without realizing that they are doing so.

Another example of a compromise of confidentiality that occurred in an EAP setting was in a large EAP. Some services had to be 'authorized for payment' when they were used. It was the crisis-counselling service that had a 'pay as you go' contract with a company. After a well-known world disaster, the company requested services for an employee and the EAP quickly provided high-quality crisis work. When the company was invoiced finance staff from the client-company queried the invoice and challenged the EAP because they had not had 'authorized payment' in advance of the service being provided. Discussion between the finance staff and the EAP had to be carried out very sensitively and the employee's consent was obtained before any further discussion took place. The finance staff wanted to know who the employee was and what was being agreed before authorization, although the EAP had quite clear contractual instructions and procedures already in position that had been followed. This eventually led to a prolonged and difficult legal argument. Meanwhile, the employee left the company half-way through the ten-session counselling contract. The company then refused to pay for the remaining five sessions that the EAP had agreed to provide to the employee after the initial assessment session. This example shows how employee-client confidentiality is not considered relevant in some companies and how bureaucratic and financial systems become more important than the counselling given to an employee. Of course, sometimes this benefit to the employee may be counter-productive for a company – such as a decision to leave, even though such a decision may be better for the employee and the company in the long run.

DUAL RELATIONSHIPS

Every workplace counsellor needs to have an understanding of 'dual relationships'. These are occupational hazards that arise when the workplace counsellor operates in a non-counselling role. One example is the workplace counsellor who has a training function as part of the service provision to employees. This is not unusual in British workplace counselling services. Depending on the size of the organization, the counsellor may be asked to deliver a training course to employees, who may include someone whom the counsellor is seeing or has previously seen as a client.

What happens when this occurs? It depends on the relationship that the counsellor and employee have or had, and it may depend on whether the employee and counsellor have discussed the possibility of seeing each other in the workplace. Some employees and some counsellors are uncomfortable with such situations. Often the counsellor may be more uneasy than the employee, as the counsellor may be more acutely aware of the boundary disturbance. However, even if the employee does not know about boundaries as a technical issue, he or she may still feel the awkwardness of the situation. Seeing a counsellor outside the safety and special milieu of the counselling room can have a dislocating effect on some clients. For a counsellor, similarly, seeing a client interacting with other employees can be an unusual and disconcerting experience. Then there is the associated problem of how the relationship between employee and counsellor is affected by an employee watching a counsellor doing something else that is not counselling. In the case of training, an employee may be watching a counsellor demonstrating in role play what the client usually sees for real. Other people may be able to work out that an employee is a client by various behaviours. For example, an employee may choose not to attend a training course on stress because he or she knows that the trainer will be his or her workplace counsellor. Other employees or managers may be able to deduce that the employee is staying away because of this. Unsubtle behaviour by an employee or workplace counsellor may give the counselling relationship away to other employees.

How do the counsellor and employee resume a counsellor–client relationship after such an experience? Should the counsellor say anything to the employee at the non-counselling event? What happens if the employee starts talking about the counselling, or if the subject matter is pertinent to the material produced in the counselling sessions? These are the types of question that can arise. Of course, a workplace counsellor, in deciding how to manage this aspect, may choose not to offer training or to participate in the life of the organization, other than by providing counselling, and then only within strict, clear boundaries.

A different problem arises when the counsellor is asked to provide counselling to a close colleague, or to an employee who has responsibilities to the counselling service or has a function that is literally or psychologically close to the counselling service. How is this discussed between counsellor and employee and to whom does the counsellor refer such a person? I return to this question in Chapter 5 where I look at the workplace counsellor's relationships with other employees.

These boundary issues are all part of being a counsellor within an organization. The various questions posed direct the focus of the counsellor to his or her role, function, access, value and position within the employing organization.

Bond (2000: 230) acknowledges that there is scant counselling literature available in Britain about dual relationships, although he recognizes (p. 35) that sometimes in the workplace dual relationships do occur, because anyone can take on the role of counsellor with appropriate training and supervision. He suggests clear demarcation between roles, and that personal relationships or professional services are not engaged in with the client simultaneously while counselling is provided. McLeod (1998: 280) identifies other relationships that fall into this category – a neighbour, a childminder and a landlord. He quotes Pope (1991), who identified that approximately 33 percent of therapists have developed relationships with clients that may be described as dual relationships, and that it happens more in the case of male therapists.

The issue has, however, been addressed by many American counsellors. The ACA includes the following statement as part of the ACA *Code of Ethics*:

A.6. Dual Relationships

a. Avoid When Possible
Counselors are aware of their influential positions with respect to clients, and they avoid exploiting the trust and dependency of clients. Counselors make every effort to avoid dual relationships with clients that could impair professional judgement or increase the risk of harm to clients. (Examples of such relationships include, but are not limited to, familial, social, financial, business or close personal relationships with clients.)

b. Superior/Subordinate Relationships.
Counselors do not accept as clients superiors or subordinates with whom they have administrative, supervisory, or evaluative relationships.

(ACA 1995: 3)

For the purposes of workplace counselling, this clear statement spells out that it is unacceptable practice to offer counselling or enter into a counselling relationship with a colleague who may be also in one of these roles.

An example from an internal EAP within a public sector organization illustrates the issue. Vito joined a local authority as a senior counsellor and was responsible for the development of counselling and EAP services for employees. He had a small caseload and referred many employees to other workplace counsellors. He developed other non-counselling services such as team development, stress audits and mentoring. He was invited to a headteachers' meeting as a guest speaker to discuss services that school employees have access to. He arrived on time, took a seat and waited for the chair of the meeting to introduce him. As he sat and waited, other headteachers arrived and sat down. After a few minutes, he realized that he recognized some of the headteachers and, as the meeting started, he counted five headteachers whom he had seen as individual employee-clients for mentoring, team development and counselling. He wondered if he should stay or go, and what would it mean if he left. He felt confused. This was a *new* relationship he had with five 'ex-clients' and he was unsure how to manage it. He decided to stay and not to acknowledge the ex-clients as clients, and the meeting continued. The ex-clients, however, all acknowledged that they had used Vito's services and added how helpful this had been for them. Struggling with some embarrassment at such public recommendation, Vito was able to enter into the spirit of the meeting – he had been invited to join in by the ex-clients, although he had never been so abruptly confronted with the issue of dual relationships before, or by so many people in one room all at once! One headteacher later admitted that she was embarrassed at the meeting as she was not sure how much she could trust some of the other headteachers, but this led to further discussion about her role in the group which she found useful. Vito quickly realized that his multiple roles would inevitably lead to such encounters, having checked it in his clinical supervision he established a more comfortable management of his different activities outside counselling.

In a BACP information sheet, 'Working in a multi-task job' (Gabriel 2002), the author refers to some of the issues about dual relationships, using the term 'multi-tasking'. An example is provided that applies to the workplace context: 'a welfare officer might provide a range of services to clients, including one-to-one contracted counselling, mediation, information giving and advocacy'. This is a common function in, and often the main source of, workplace counselling. However, as Gabriel explains, in these circumstances:

work practices, boundaries and lines of communication can sometimes be unclear and consequently, anxiety and conflict about role identity and responsibilities can arise. Dealing with the multiple functions involved in the job can be stressful. Problems can be compounded when a practitioner's theoretical orientation and clinical approach conflict with the organisation's approach or expectation.

(2002: 5)

Such problems may not be easy to predict, but if the workplace counsellor sets out his or her boundaries to the organization as he or she would with an individual employee before starting counselling, some of these problems may not arise. However, the ability to contain change, unpredictability and conflict of interests are all part of the challenge of being a workplace counsellor. The counsellor will be thoroughly tested in some organizations whether he or she becomes part of the organization, remains outside of it or rides the complex boundary in between.

EVALUATION

Measuring the value of a psychological process has been difficult from the beginning of the 'talking cure'. Evaluating the possible benefits of psychotherapy has been a tortuous task that has required designing and borrowing measurement tools that are in many ways alien to the sensitive, demanding and patient tasks of psychotherapeutic intervention. Evaluating counselling today is as difficult as it was when Freud was developing his techniques. Towards the end of his career Freud assessed the results of analysis in terms of curing his patients of their neuroses by 'replacing insecure repressions by reliable and ego-syntonic controls' ([1937] 2001: 331).

The aim of psychotherapy is to bring about a change in the personality of the patient so that the patient can be 'released from neurotic hangovers (pathogenic defenses) and can confront the realistic problems of his life as a mature human being' (Munro 1956: 323). If the aim is clear then there is a possibility of establishing if the treatment has been successful through evaluation.

When describing the alliance made between analyst and patient, Freud outlined his intention:

Our plan of cure is based upon these views. The ego has been weakened by the internal conflict; we must come to its aid. The

position is like a civil war which can only be decided by the help
of an ally from without. The analytical physician and the weakened ego of the patient, basing themselves upon the real
external world, are to combine against the enemies, the
instinctual demands of the id and the moral demands of the
super-ego. We form a pact with each other. The patient's sick ego
promises us the most complete candour, promises that is, to put
at our disposal all the material which his self-perception provides; we on the other hand, assure him of the strictest discretion
and put at his service our experience in interpreting material
that has been influenced by the unconscious. Our knowledge
shall compensate for his ignorance and shall give his ego once
more mastery over the lost provinces of his mental life. This pact
constitutes the analytic situation.

([1938] 2001: 36)

Freud acknowledged that not all the results were favourable and that
this process was not always complete. He frequently had to defend
his method, and this helped him to re-evaluate the effectiveness of
the talking cure he had developed. His process of careful, patient
listening and helping an individual to further their understanding
of their lives is still the aim of most forms of counselling and
psychotherapy today. But the problem is how are these aims actually
evaluated and measured?

There are now more sophisticated tools for assessing outcome and
psychological change. The use of single case studies, developed by
Freud as an explanation of the treatment, has been enriched by the
application of empirical methods to provide clearer understanding of
the process of counselling and therapy. Mander (2000) cites Malan
as one major radical contributor to the scientific development of
psychodynamic theory and practice, although research into efficacy
was part of behavioural and cognitive-behavioural therapy from the
start.

Since Freud's time, more people in organizations have an active
interest in how a process is measured. The era of 'evidence-based
practice' arrived in the United Kingdom several years ago, leading to
many questions that need to be asked about how services are evaluated. Some managers may want to be able to produce tangible results
that prove the efficiency of introducing counselling services, in the
same way that they may want to justify the purchase of a new
photocopier.

Can a counselling service be evaluated by non-counsellors, by
those who are responsible for funding it? In most organizations that

have a workplace counselling service or use an EAP the evaluation of the service is indeed carried out by non-counselling managers.

It obviously makes sense for counsellors to evaluate their own service, but how do the outcomes of the workplace counsellor match the outcomes required by the organization? What happens if a service is not evaluated? What are the motives for evaluation? Evaluation may be an ordinary function, a health check to monitor reality, but there are nonetheless anxieties and fantasies connected to this 'ordinary' function.

There is a debate about evaluation of counselling in the general counselling world that is reflected in workplace counselling. However, because of the specific context of workplace counselling there is perhaps more readiness for workplace counsellors to evaluate their services. If everything else around them gets measured, why should they not be measured too? Some counsellors and counsellor commentators believe that counselling can be evaluated and should be. Their opponents believe that measurement is impossible and irrelevant to counselling. It is clear that some counsellors and providers of counselling services in the workplace do not see evaluation as part of their responsibility, and it is not a major issue for them. As Cooper and Highley-Marchington put it: 'Providers and counsellors frequently do not see evaluation as part of their mission. By virtue of their professional training and commitment, they have confidence in the efficacy of their work' (1998: 13).

Measurement appears to be a dirty word to some people in the field of counselling and psychotherapy. It is certainly not something many counsellors feel able to do. Robinson (2002) explores some of these issues from her perspective as a psychoanalytic psychotherapist in an NHS trust and sees 'problems in applying numbers to psychotherapy'. She states her concerns that 'an over-indulgence in measures will make what gets counted count because practitioners are intelligent enough to devise ways to respond to ensure that they are regarded as successful, making their numbers and statistics fit the prescribed standards' (2002: 52). O'Carroll (2002) follows a similar line of argument and believes that a 'new kind of earnest bureaucrat has lately appeared among us. Having bought the myth of science as the most noble enterprise our species has invented, this official designs questionnaires whose purpose is to show that the client benefits from the time he [sic] spends in a specific kind of dialogue' (2002: 11).

Although many counsellors will say that they have an aversion to figures and statistics, many are sufficiently organizationally aware and astute enough to make the figures work in their favour. And according to Cooper and Highley-Marchington this is essential:

The importance of evaluating an EAP cannot be overestimated.
Many programmes must be evaluated to justify their existence
to some external authority. Even if this is not the case, an EAP
should be evaluated, or at least audited, to ascertain the extent to
which it is reaching its objectives and to find ways to improve
the effectiveness of its performance. The goals of an EAP should
be built in from the beginning and it is essential for organisations
to be able to evaluate whether or not those goals are being met.

(1998: 99)

These two authors found some interesting facts about organizations
and evaluation: 45 percent of EAPs/counselling services that were
involved in their report said that they had been audited or evaluated,
but this was not true, they had not been audited in any 'systematic
and independent way' (1998: 90). From their research, it was also
clear that many organizations had no clear understanding about
audit or evaluation of these services.

It is not only some counsellors that resist measurement. Many
EAPs and workplace counselling services do not carry out any evaluation of their services in any depth, and as a whole the workplace
counselling and the EAP industry in the United Kingdom lack any
significant research into evaluation and utilization. Much of the
research that EAPs have produced is self-congratulatory, and usually
proves that an EAP is a good idea for an employer. McLeod (2001:
93) states that research 'has not been able to find any consistent link
between EAP/counselling provision and organizational outcomes
such as job satisfaction, commitment and productivity'. Yet job satisfaction, commitment and productivity are usually the main focus for
selling a service to an employer.

McLeod suggests that longer periods of time may be necessary to
obtain true data and significant information producing a depth of
understanding about the value of workplace counselling, because
employees take long periods of time to use and benefit from it. The
impact of a counselling service on an employee's work performance
may not be seen by an employer for many months or years.

McLeod's report is crucial to the debate about evaluation. In order
to find some clarity, and because of the methodological difficulties
that pervade the whole subject area, he divides his report into three
main categories: best evidence, supporting evidence and authenticat-
ing evidence (2001: 17). He has created a hierarchy of studies. Objective, relevant studies constitute the best evidence, and descriptive,
qualitative studies constitute authenicating evidence. The other
valuable structure McLeod uses when assessing these studies is the

differentiation of outcome into psycho-social outcomes, economic outcomes and employee utilization outcomes. This is because there are many possible outcomes and evaluations of workplace counselling services.

Briner (2000) adds another challenging and critical voice to the debate about evaluation, arguing that orthodox measurements of EAP effectiveness are over-simplified and that there is 'evidence and theory that they may not "work" in the way they are claimed to work'. He suggests that there are other more complex successes that EAPs have but that they are not adequately measured. This may be because the benefits that he identifies are the changes in an employee's team or co-workers that are brought about by one employee having counselling for personal concerns. He calls this 'emotional contagion' (2000: 3). He also writes: 'Individual perform-ance of the client is only minimally reduced as a consequence of their personal concerns but this very small performance reduction has a major knock-on effect on co-workers and removing it will have large effects on co-workers' (2000: 2). He adds: 'An employee experi-encing negative affect may negatively influence the mood of others and hence improving an employee's feelings may also improve the feelings of their co-workers' (2000: 3).

These are some of the benefits that line managers receive from EAPs. They also benefit by feeling more secure about helping employees, knowing that there are external sources of assistance, which reduce the amount of time they need to spend themselves in helping employees with personal concerns. These benefits are not usually looked at in evaluating the effectiveness of EAPs, but there is a

> need for a theoretical framework which draws on best available theory and evidence about work and well-being in order to bet-ter understand: possible multiple and complex effects of EAPs, how EAPs integrate and interact with other organisational prac-tices, how and in what ways they may work, how and in what ways they may *not* work
>
> (Briner: 2000)

Work performance may be another indicator for evaluating an EAP/counselling service. Arthur (2001) gives an example of how an EAP wanted to examine its effectiveness and asked itself an interesting question: what was the level of psychological disturbance of employees using the EAP? The answer was shocking but useful for the EAP. The client companies were asked to participate, and the results from employees using the service showed that '87 per cent were experiencing significant psychiatric trouble' (Arthur 2001). One of the inferences from this study is that a large number of employees using British EAPs may be experiencing serious mental health problems and are using their EAP rather than other community medical/psychological services.

The EAPA has some general guidelines for evaluation. It emphasizes the need to evaluate: 'The importance of evaluation should not be overlooked as "evaluation empowers the purchaser". Purchasers should expect some form of evaluation from providers as a matter of course' (EAPA UK 1998: 10).

The EAPA has also tried to suggest a formula for measuring utilization rates of EAP services by organizations. One of the reasons for doing this was because it was 'impossible to compare programs and conduct benchmarking surveys . . . EAP activity must be counted accurately and fully so that both employers and EAP professionals can understand the value of their Employee Assistance programs' (EAPA UK 2002).

Amaral (1999: 161) makes an important point about benchmarking and EAP provision for an organization: what gets left out of the benchmarking process risks being devalued or simply not counted, so it is essential for the EAP world to begin to design and implement practical benchmarking tools to align EAPs with all the other measurable aspects of organizations.

Oher (1999: 117) offers an evaluation tool that was designed to help an organization make important decisions about the effectiveness of its EAP when it was facing financial hardship and was contemplating cutting back or ending the EAP contract. The survey developed was not scientific, Oher points out, and was based on a small number of returns from HR managers using the service. However, the data collected highlighted (1999: 119):

- Service satisfaction.
- Factors in the decision to use/not use services.
- Recommended service changes.
- Types of problem for which employees and management utilized the programme.
- Effectiveness of services relative to their key components.
- Programme confidentiality.
- User demographics.
- Correlation between programme use and changes in employee behaviour.

Some of the results showed that the organization did not have clear views on what was expected from the EAP to begin with; that most of the users of the service valued it; and a surprising and contradictory issue arose about confidentiality: most users did not know if the service was confidential but used the service because they thought it was.

The lack of agreement about evaluation means that measurement of outcomes, of services provided and of any other results of counselling interventions, is essentially random. Because of this ambiguity, results that are published or released are difficult to compare or to benchmark in a scientific manner. Cooper and Highley-Marchington (1998: 14) put this reluctance down to a variety of factors: commercial competition, confidentiality; the uniqueness of each EAP, which is tailored to the specific needs of an organization; lack of cooperation between providers; reasons for establishing an EAP within an organization; personal interest of employees who promote and establish the use of an EAP; and the desire for privacy by some organizations, not wanting the public to perceive them as having any problems.

There is a further phenomenon in the United Kingdom that has an impact upon the evaluation debate – evidence-based practice. Evidence-based practice is part of everyday working life for many counsellors working in the NHS. Goss and Rose (2002) outline the challenge of evidence-based practice that counselling and psychotherapy services in Britain are having to face. Initiated by the Cochrane Collaboration, many sectors of service in the NHS have now to prove that the best possible evidence is used in making decisions about treatment and services, rather than simply the opinion of experts. Counsellors in primary healthcare settings are familiar with the philosophy and language associated with these ideals, and are incorporating best evidence of their practice into their daily work. Goss and Rose emphasize the need for counsellors to keep up to date with counselling research and to develop a critical eye to distinguish between good and bad research. This will enable counsellors to enhance their practices and establish counselling that is based upon the best information available. Another major element in this development is the problem that counsellors will face if they choose a course of action or pursue a method of working with a client that is contrary to the best evidence available and clinical practice guidelines. Although not compulsory, these guidelines are increasingly important to counsellors.

The most comprehensive and systematic evaluation of counselling services in the United Kingdom is known as CORE (Clinical Outcome in Routine Evaluation). It is of cardinal importance for workplace counselling. CORE is a standardized evaluation system, developed by a multi-disciplinary group of researchers for use within the NHS (Mellor-Clark *et al.* 1999). More recently, it has been expanded and developed to fit workplace counselling services (Mellor-Clark 2002). The aim of this modification was to provide a national database for workplace counselling evaluation and benchmarking. Mellor-Clark's starting point is a series of questions for organizations, managers of counselling services and EAPs: what is there in place to protect the employee-client in the service? And what is there in place to protect the employee-client from the counsellor? He believes that, in the *zeitgeist* of accountability that pervades most work domains, it is increasingly difficult to justify the provision of counselling 'behind a closed door'. This is a powerful image and points to a question that is being asked of counsellors, one which challenges to some extent the essence of the working alliance and the therapeutic relationship: can counsellors become more transparent about what they do with clients in the consulting room? Mellor-Clark suggests that the performance of counsellors and psychotherapists has to be measurable, because we have to learn more about why all 'outcomes' in therapy are not equally successful (Mellor-Clark 2002). He acknowledges that evaluations are done regularly by many workplace counsellors, but there is not much investigation into the clients who do not appear to have benefited from counselling. We know, for example, that the research shows that counselling works for a large number of clients: 'Two-thirds of studies have shown that, following counselling, levels of work-related symptoms and stress return to the "normal" range for more than 50% of clients' (McLeod 2001: 4). But what about the third of reports that do not show improvement and the 50 percent of clients who have not returned to 'normal'? Is it possible to investigate these figures, learn from those clients who do not benefit and explore the operations of a service to improve these figures? One reason it is difficult is because clients who cancel their counselling appointments are usually reluctant to provide any further information that may be useful to the counsellor or the EAP. However, this is an area for much more exploration by workplace counsellors, and the CORE system is an effective tool that can help counsellors understand their impact on clients.

Supported by CORE, the system processes qualitative data into quantitative data and then returns the information to qualitative data in a loop-like process. The whole of the CORE system revolves around this method; the practitioner and the employee-client fill in three forms in total, before and after the agreed number of counselling sessions. The information is collated and the client's 'scores' are matched against clinical 'norms' generated by NHS-based research

(CORE System Group 1998). This gives an instant picture that can tell the counsellor how the client matches the 'norm' before and after counselling. These 'norms' were developed from data collected from two sources – a mixed non-clinical group of university students and convenience sample, and an NHS clinical group undergoing various psychological interventions (Evans *et al*. 2002).

Used in the workplace, the yield from such a tool is impressive – it provides an immediate image of the psychological health of the employee. Further details are provided about the client and also about the caseload of individual counsellors. The information about individual counsellor's caseload is particularly interesting as it shows how their clients have progressed. The use of CORE in workplace services is now slowly being expanded following an early pilot study that involved ten workplace counselling services collecting evaluative information from 2500 employee-clients (Mellor-Clark 2001b). Highlights of this study showed that workplace counselling services varied widely along service quality dimensions (Mellor-Clark and Barkham 2000), not only when compared with each other but also within the same service. For example, in a mix of NHS and workplace counselling services, this efficiency measure (clients attending planned appointments) varied between services from 65 percent to 95 percent. This means that in some of the services clients attend 95 percent of the appointments offered, but in others only 65 percent. Why is there such variation? Mellor-Clark makes if clear that if the information supplied by CORE is not used to improve the services to employees, organizations and the working lives of counsellors then much of the evaluation is wasted (Mellor-Clark 2001b). Counsellors need managing, and management can be used to better counselling services to employee-clients. This theme is returned to in Chapter 4.

The key benefits of the CORE system are two-fold. First, the CORE outcome measure assesses counselling *effectiveness* by pre- and post-therapy comparison. Second, the practitioner-completed therapy assessment form and end of therapy form profile *resource efficiency*, by highlighting unattended appointments; *equity of access*, by identifying client demographics relative to the workplace population; *accessibility*, described by appointment waiting times; *appropriateness*, by identifying concurrent and/or previous therapy; and *acceptability*, determined by clients' unplanned endings. Thus, collectively, the evaluation system helps to give a comprehensive service quality profile of what is on offer to employees and the usage of the service. More information is available from the CORE website (http://www.coreims.co.uk).

There is some resistance to introducing CORE into commercial services as the information is revealing about organizations and employees as well as about EAPs and counsellors. Also, there are problems with the system; the client is asked to complete the questionnaires and, no matter how cooperative they may have been during counselling, some clients will not complete them, or they do not return them to the counselling service, and some counsellors may 'interfere' with the questionnaires. Carroll (1996: 145), pre-dating CORE, highlights the tensions and various disagreements that have developed between counsellors about giving clients such forms, as some counsellors believe the forms interfere with the sensitive process of helping a vulnerable client to communicate. Nevertheless, CORE is an important aspect of the evolution of counselling in the United Kingdom and may in the future help counselling to become even safer and more effective for client and counsellor.

There are, then, different views about evaluation in the UK counselling world, there are different commercial pressures and there is a culture of secrecy that inhibits a national commercial standard for evaluation, but evidence-based practice in the NHS will increasingly have an impact on counsellors in workplace settings as more counsellors become familiar and comfortable with routine evaluation of their work.

Carroll writes the following about evaluation:

> Evaluation is a key element in counselling provision. Not only is it a way of ensuring that clients are receiving services that are being monitored for their effectiveness, but it is also a way of convincing purchasers about the value of the service. Furthermore, evaluation, through in-depth analysis of what is happening, can be a worthwhile means of improving services.
>
> (1996: 134)

To summarize, there are different reasons for evaluation, such as the statistical, and different foci for it: clients, counsellors, organizations, supervisors, process and outcome. Carroll concludes: 'Fundamental to good evaluation in workplace counselling is clear agreement on *what* is being evaluated' (1996: 148). He goes on to ask simple questions (1996: 148) such as why, who, what, where, how and when will evaluation take place, questions on which, in conclusion, we will elaborate.

Why evaluate a counselling service? A workplace counselling service does not have to be evaluated since there are no legal requirements to do so, nor are there moral imperatives that make evaluation essential. There are services that have very little evaluation in terms of the individual counselling relationships or how the service meets the organizational objectives, and its absence does not necessarily make these services less effective. The effectiveness of the service is sometimes communicated by word of mouth, which reaches the ears of managers who are then satisfied with the service. However, in that case one wonders at the absence of negative feedback. It may be that the service is quite well established in the organization, is successful, integrated and effective, and that negative feedback does not occur. Yet the lack of formal evaluation may mask aspects of the service which could be improved.

There are no sanctions or requirements that are enforceable by the main counselling bodies in the United Kingdom regarding evaluation, although the importance of research is stressed in the BACP's *Ethical Framework* (2002). There are also expectations that services will want to evaluate their effectiveness. The guidelines and rules of the counselling bodies do not always equate with moral imperatives, and it is clear that some services do not evaluate their product in any systematic or structured sense. They believe that what they provide works and that they would hear from clients if it did not work. They assume their whole attention is needed for the work with the clients, not for what they see as administering pedantic, unnecessary and overly bureaucratic statistics. One of the problems with evaluation in the counselling world is anxiety on the part of some counsellors who are afraid that their work will not be understood, or that their work will not be good enough for the employing body.

Other services take the opposite view, seeing themselves as being like any other department, to be measured and evaluated to determine how effectively they meet the primary objectives determined by the organization. Managers of these services wonder what there is to be afraid of in evaluation. These services have a form of evaluation that helps to maintain their profile within their employing body, presented to non-counsellor managers in managerial language, in an annual or quarterly report. The emphasis in these reports is usually on how important the service is to the organization, the level of serious psychological disturbance they are dealing with, the numbers of employees seen, the successful outcomes of the counselling provided and how many employees have been kept at work by the service. Reports are compiled from feedback sheets from employees, statistics gathered by the counsellors and administrators, and other information that the service managers gather from within the organization. These documents legitimize, authenticate and position the counselling services. They can promote the visibility of the service to managers and decision-makers who otherwise might not be aware of its existence.

Whatever the resistances may be towards evaluation, and no

matter what the difficulties are in trying to evaluate psychological phenomena, Leiper (2000) reminds us that evaluation is a normal part of modern work life. 'If experience is the food of learning, then evaluation is the digestive process' (2000: 197). Without frequent evaluations, we are less able able to make informed decisions or judgements. Evaluation is a reflective process that is essential for individuals and organizations.

Who will evaluate the service? It might be the counsellors, the client-employees, the trade unions or elected representatives, the counsellor-manager, the human resources department, the CEO or senior management, or an outside body that has an understanding of EAPs/workplace counselling – or a combination of any of these.

What will be evaluated? Carroll (1996) suggests it should be clear from the outset what the service is meant to provide and how this will be measured. It may be a subjective measure from employees and counsellors, or an objective measure against yardsticks such as sickness absenteeism, employee turnover and productivity. It may be purely statistical – such as the numbers of employees using the service, gender, presenting problems and so on. It may look at results set against what it costs to run the service or, again, a combination of any of these.

Where in the organization will the evaluation be positioned? Included here is the question of location of the service, as discussed in Chapter 2. Evaluation may say something to the organization about both the geographical and psychological position of the service, and whether the service is sufficiently visible.

When is the right time to evaluate a service? Should client feedback be part of evaluation, based upon their feedback at the end of their counselling? I have shown how some counsellors are unhappy with this, and differences in counsellor orientation certainly determine how a counsellor reacts to this part of the work. A counsellor using mainly cognitive-behavioural techniques with a client has a different perspective on asking the client to evaluate agreed aims and outcomes to that of a counsellor using a mainly psychodynamic approach. Outcomes of counselling are also determined by expectations raised by the assessment, the therapeutic orientation of the counsellor, readiness of the client to engage in a difficult process and, to some degree, by other people or influences such as the setting and environment, the waiting list and organizational factors. There are also questions about the best time to evaluate a service, such as annually, quarterly or monthly.

CONCLUSION

In this chapter I have examined three features of workplace counselling that are of particular importance to the setting up and maintenance of an effective service. There are other issues that are significant to the workplace counsellor, which I examine in Chapter 4.

· FOUR ·

Specific issues in workplace counselling

Despite the fact that the analytic setting is of importance in the therapeutic equation, it cannot replace psychoanalytic technique: the art of interpretation, and the skill in relating to a human being.

(Greenson 1967: 410)

One of the most striking differences between analytic practice and workplace counselling is the physical setting, although as Greenson (1967) suggests, whatever the setting, the most important aspects of the therapy are the fundamental skills of listening to and understanding another person.

There are other important differences between workplace counselling, private practice and counselling in other contexts. Some of the differences, such as the function of case management in EAPs and some workplace counselling services, may be obvious to experienced counsellors, but I think more depth can be added to the debate. Some differences are not acknowledged or recognized by some counsellors and counselling organizations, such as the absence of fees for workplace counselling, and this is an area that I am especially interested in. This chapter outlines the major differences that define workplace counselling as a specific form.

SETTING

The setting defines counselling on many important levels. I am referring initially to the *physical* setting. Some workplace counselling services deliberately try to make their physical environment look inconspicuous, ordinary and anonymous in order to help employees access the service. If a service identifies itself in a large, bold and 'loud' physical sense, this may deter employees from approaching the counselling department, consulting room or building. It is important for a service to proclaim its presence within an organization, advertising that it is there and that it delivers a confidential service, and so on, but this need not be repeated at the door into the service. Discretion of the counselling setting is vital in the workplace, but cannot always be guaranteed. I know of one service in a large public sector organization that does not have a dedicated counselling room. The counsellor has to book rooms in advance for meeting employees. These rooms are often not ideal and sometimes an employee may be seen by colleagues entering or leaving a room; sometimes colleagues may even be able to see the counsellor in the room with the client.

Many employees do not want to be seen entering or leaving a workplace counselling service. They are wary about being seen by others as they access the service and this may add to their anxiety about the whole counselling process. There are other considerations about the setting: the client may overhear or see secretarial staff or even other clients. The consulting rooms may be poorly sound-proofed and may have windows or glazing that expose the client. The client may have to go to different rooms for subsequent sessions.

Client's records/notes may be visible to other employees/staff. Care needs to be taken with counselling notes or files, as in some settings the counsellor may have more than one consulting room or office. The counsellor may be peripatetic and therefore the security of notes/files needs careful attention. Wherever the counsellor is based, the notes/files must be stored securely with access limited to that counsellor. There may be other parties who are involved with a client's care in a clinic and this may also apply in the workplace – such as line managers, secretaries, colleagues, occupational health personnel and so on. For example, a personnel officer may have referred a member of staff for counselling prior to referring the employee for a medical report. The referral for counselling may require a limited report back to the personnel officer, with the employee's consent, before a medical report is requested. Understanding and managing these boundaries is part of the function and setting for many workplace counsellors.

The client may find himself or herself engaged in conversations with work colleagues about the counselling service, which may include reports about the counsellor that can be positive or negative, or there might be comments about those who go for counselling, especially where the need for counselling is seen as a sign of weakness.

All of these concerns about the setting affect the counselling relationship and process, and can sometimes be recognized in a client's lateness, absence, early departure from sessions and, occasionally, complaints about the counsellor, as well as many other client deviations within the session. An example of how the setting intrudes upon and even forms the counselling relationship to some extent, can be taken from my experience of one large local authority. Here the employee-clients have to access the consulting rooms via a main reception. They have to ask for a security card from the receptionists to pass through security barriers to get to the consulting rooms. Often the reception area is busy and sometimes the employee-clients have to wait for the receptionist to give them a card. This delays the employee-client getting to the counsellor. Sometimes this delay is commented on by the employee. The counsellor describes how getting through the security barrier is a useful analogy for some clients, as this is parallel to their problems in seeking assistance, and how remote the counsellor may seem and to the hurdles that the employee has to overcome before he or she can start to talk. However, to other employee-clients it is a distraction; it feels like a compromise to their anonymity and they complain to the counsellor. The counsellor may also be affected by these concerns and find that he or she behaves differently. For example, the local authority counsellor above says that in his private practice, where there is no security barrier to the consultation room, he will challenge lateness and delays more readily. As employees have difficulty accessing the room because of the setting, he is more accepting of their 'real' reasons for delay and does not labour an interpretation, unless the employee-client seems over-interested in the delay caused by the barrier. The setting intrudes in a real way for these employees and the counsellor. The communicative psychotherapist Robert Langs is very firm on the need for a secure frame and, of course, in this setting 'time, frequency and duration of sessions, are . . . likely to be compromised' (1998: 137). However, despite these problems and challenges Langs acknowledges that if the basic ground rules for counselling are established, even when there are disrupted and deviant settings, clients can still benefit from profound insights gained with the help of counsellors and therapists.

Many workplace counselling rooms and EAP facilities are far from ideal. But useful 'therapeutic' work can take place in most unusual or bizarre settings. For example, a discussion between a workplace counsellor and an employee at a drinks machine may be all that is needed for the employee to feel confident enough to subsequently telephone and make an appointment with the counsellor. Or a manager may ask a question of the counsellor in a corridor which leads to a referral from the manager, or to a connection that assists the manager to assess the value of the counsellor. 'Corridor conversations' are often vital to a counsellor's profile within an organization, and these informal referral meetings, assessments of the counsellor and other ways of 'checking out' form an essential part not only of the integration process of the counsellor into the organization, but of her or his on-going presence. Of course, it is not just referral and assessment that occurs, counselling on the spot can be sought by some employees. This is where the workplace counsellor has to have a firm sense of the basic counselling ground rules and boundaries in order to avoid being pulled into 'frame-less' settings. It is often employees who are ignorant of the specific conditions required for counselling who do this, but occasionally employees with full awareness of counselling conditions unconsciously try to pull the counsellor out of role when they see the counsellor out of their usual setting. One workplace counsellor describes this further:

> When I am out of my counselling room, perhaps going to the toilet, getting my lunch from my car, or going to a meeting I am visible to a large number of employees in the corridors of the building going about their day-to-day business. Sometimes I feel exposed, too visible! Perhaps this is a slightly paranoid feeling, but I wonder who I will meet – clients, managers, occupational health people etc? I don't think I scurry when out of my room, but I wouldn't be surprised if I look a bit furtive in my movements around the building!

There is a 'caged animal' feeling in this description – can the counsellor scurry back to the safety of his room without being waylaid by a number of other people? The counsellor needs to feel secure in the setting as much as the client/employee does, and this often occurs during this more public exposure.

Examples of safe settings include the counselling rooms at Longton Hospital, Stoke, the Hampshire County Council, the Calm Service at Astra Zeneca and some of the rooms at the ICAS premises. These rooms are all quiet, free from external noise and unobtrusive – they are discreet in their position in the building, simply furnished, comfortable, with natural light but not overlooked or looked into from external sources, warm without being stuffy and hot, and free from telephones, computers or other office equipment. Some of them have small bookcases that contain a selection of self-help books and counselling textbooks.

Workplace counsellors can provide this type of setting, and no doubt there are other organizations in the UK that spend time and money on establishing a suitable environment for the counsellors. But some workplace counsellors have to make do with what is given.

To compensate for such settings, workplace counsellors have to rely even more heavily on their adherence to basic ground rules and upon their own containment of the client. Provided that the counsellor is aware of the effort they have to make to counter the problems that may arise in such deviant settings, successful counselling and beneficial therapeutic relationships can still be achieved.

CASE MANAGEMENT

The next fundamental aspect of workplace counselling is the function of case management. This usually forms part of the organizational administration and clinical containment of employees and is found within EAP and workplace settings. In private practice there are usually three parties involved in the counselling process; the client, the counsellor and the counsellor's supervisor. In workplace counselling there are usually four parties: the employee-client, the counsellor, the counsellor's supervisor and the employer. The employer's role in the counselling process will vary depending upon the nature of the organization and depending upon the organization's interest and/or the need for information about the counselling process. But in any situation where an EAP is used, the organization will be 'present' in the counselling through the function of the EAP case management process.

Case management is more than a bureaucratic function that watches and monitors the activity of the counsellor with a client, although it is still a popular belief in some quarters of the counselling population that this is its only function. Case management can be a benign clinical container for the organization, counsellor and client when it works correctly and is understood by all involved.

The EAPA define EAP case management as follows:

> Case management protects the interests of both the client and the purchasing organisation by ensuring that the service delivered remains within the boundaries of the agreed contract. It protects the quality and continuity of care to the client, continues to support the EA counsellor or other professional in

relation to the particular workplace context and explores options and liabilities in relation to both the purchasing organisation's expectations and the client's needs.

(EAPA UK 2000: 51)

This definition makes a distinction between case management and clinical supervision. The people who provide case management for counsellors should have adequate and appropriate experience and training, have access to clinical specialists, have regular contact with the counsellor in connection to the client in the process and be able to feed back appropriate information to the employee's organization. In addition, if an emergency occurs with a client, the case manager will be able to follow an agreed protocol to support the employee and the counsellor – for example, if an employee indicates suicidal intention, the protocol will help all three parties (the case manager, employee and counsellor) to manage the situation. Finally, the EAPA recommends that case managers help workplace counsellors comply with best practice as determined by national bodies such as the BACP, ensuring that counsellors do not work with client caseloads over the recommended limits.

The EAPA suggests that case management 'is welcomed by most EAP affiliates. It enables them to share the realities of each case with an experienced colleague who has additional information about the continuity of appropriate care for the client and about the culture, policies and other contractual expectations of the purchasing organisation' (EAPA UK 2000: 52).

There are different case management models used by EAPs to fit the needs of the client-companies and the particular philosophy of the individual EAP. There appears not to be a universal case management model and this is not surprising, but it could be something for the future, if EAPs desire more universal understanding of what they provide.

The British counselling community is as split over the issue of case management as it is over the similar problem of evaluation. There are arguments on both sides about the function of monitoring, evaluation and case management, which question the whole purpose of counselling. Munt (2000: 419) refers to EAP systems that 'require time-consuming paperwork tasks to be done without payment', further, he states that counsellors involved in EAP work find 'themselves increasingly corralled into corporate, bureaucratic systems and structures of the very kind they may have trained in counselling and entered private practice to avoid'. This is an important statement about counsellors' commercial vulnerability that is revisited in Chapter 6.

However, there have been serious legal problems faced by some counsellors in organizations concerning the monitoring of the counselling process, the counsellor–client relationship and outcomes of counselling. Bond (2000: 214) outlines the difficulties experienced by student counsellors, providing counselling for students in a higher education setting, when government-appointed education inspectors are asked to sit in and observe counselling sessions to monitor the quality of this activity. Eventually, in the early 1990s the then Association of Student Counsellors, supported by the BAC, arrived at a resolution that such observation invalidates what is being observed, undermines the counsellor's promise of confidentiality and that freely given client consent may be very difficult to determine in the setting. This is an example of how difficult it can be to find a relevant and sensitive system of understanding the counselling relationship.

One EAP manager said that the most vulnerable part of any EAP that offers face to face counselling is the counselling session that takes place between counsellor and employee. The EAP has to rely completely upon the training, integrity and personality of the counsellor. The EAP has to trust the counsellor absolutely to provide what is required in the manner that the EAP prefers, without compromising the employee, the client-company, the EAP or the counsellor. These are sophisticated boundaries and demands that are made upon all involved in the counselling, and are part of the reason EAPs provide training to clarify the counsellor's role and function in the EAP.

Sonnenstuhl (1986: 113) makes an important observation about the recruitment of therapists to a particular corporate counselling service – the company was able to select therapists 'whose interests coincide with those of the company'; he adds that these therapists were sufficiently clinically experienced and mature enough (30–35 years old) 'not to disrupt the company's work' (1986: 113). The senior management of this company had very little 'managerial' interest in the therapists' clinical work, and regular clinical supervision was provided by the director of the service, but the management were interested in the provision of the service to the organization. Essentially, the therapists were trusted. This is not to suggest that case management is a function evolved from distrust of therapists, although this may be how it is perceived by some counsellors. In this example the careful selection of the therapists appears to have obviated the need for case management. I return to this issue in Chapter 5.

There are a variety of case management models in use. The nature of the organization, the originally identified requirements for counselling and the accounting/managerial needs of the organization all influence the type of case management developed. An example is the case management used in one NHS staff counselling service. There case management is carefully differentiated from supervision and is carried out verbally by the manager of the staff counselling service once a fortnight with each counsellor. The manager uses these discussions to check how the counsellor is assessing risks with employee-clients, to explore any breaches of confidentiality that may occur and to assess the need for more sessions requested by the counsellor, beyond the fixed number of sessions. Case management helps the counselling service integrate with other internal and external services; for example, in one case an employee, referred for counselling by a trade union representative, was suffering from domestic violence and the aggressor had already threatened to attack the counsellor. This was discussed in the case management session and steps were taken to ensure the safety of the counsellor and the employee. Case management in this setting is one part of a continuum of care that extended from the trade union, through the staff counselling service and eventually to the psychiatric service, which in this case further helped this employee. The organization in this example has an 'At Risk Protocol' for service users (its customers) which in this instance was extended to the employee. Through discussion in case management, with the employee's consent, the counsellor and counselling service staff were able to contact the police, take the employee to the Accident and Emergency Department and arrange for psychiatric assessment and/ or care.

The counsellors in this service report positively about case management, as it helps the manager have an idea about what is going on. It has a focused function and is generally helpful. One counsellor, relatively new to organizational settings, reported the support from the process as being very useful in terms of being able to tell his manager directly about how he is coping with the number of cases he has and the variety of issues he is helping clients with. Case management helps these counsellors to feel part of the staff counselling team, and this in turn integrates the staff counselling service into the larger organization. It creates a feeling that is distinct from supervision as it has an organizational slant and there is a manager–subordinate dynamic that is absent in private practice and a number of other settings.

Some case management systems operate upon informal verbal reports from the counsellor to the case manager. Often the case manager is the manager of the service, or coordinator of a counselling service. Some use a more formal structure for recording and checking the counselling process. This is often based upon a dialogue between a counsellor and a designated 'case manager'.

THE ABSENCE OF FEES

The meaning of money and the fee

A fascinating and vital difference between workplace counselling and private practice setting is the absence of fees paid by the client to the counsellor. There are other settings where this is also a factor (for example, counselling in the health service and in education), but in the workplace this is a specific dynamic, often unconscious and critically relevant to defining workplace counselling. Money and our relation to money may tell us everything we may want to know about ourselves, our lives and our relationships. Money is a commodity that client and counsellor both need. It is an important part of the relationship between counsellor and client and requires careful attention in private practice. Any subtle nuances about fees that the counsellor may detect from the client can lead to an exploration of useful, rich material that illuminates other aspects of the client's personality. Feelings about money and about the fee for counselling are communicated from the very beginning of the client–counsellor relationship. These feelings sometimes reveal other issues. The fee is a real object that belongs to the real world but it can be laden with complex and powerful meanings.

This is quite obvious in Freud's recommendation of a frank no-nonsense approach to the fee: he believed that this approach to money would assist in encouraging frank discussion about sexual matters! He observed 'the value of treatment is not enhanced in the patient's eyes if a very low fee is asked' ([1913] 2001: 352). Providing free treatment for patients 'enormously increases many neurotic resistances', he writes, concluding: 'The absence of the corrective influence in payment of the professional fee is felt as a serious handicap; the whole relationship recedes into an unreal world; and the patient is deprived of a useful incentive to exert himself to bring the cure to an end' ([1913] 2001: 353).

But clearly this is very different in settings where no fee is charged. Without the necessity of financial commitment to counselling many employee-clients have different experiences of their therapist, regardless of the therapist's counselling orientation, the number of sessions, the outcome of therapy and so on. If the therapy is free, the relationship between therapist and employee-client in some situations can be devalued. The client can take or leave it, the value is inconsequential and the client can afford to be indifferent. Of course, this may be a form of resistance against the therapy that a client uses to demean and ward off the difficult tasks faced in therapy. This is much easier to do if the therapist is perceived as offering something free in the first instance. In establishing a 'free at point of contact' service to help employees and give them free counselling, resistances preventing use of the service may therefore quickly be established. If it is free, what values are initially attributed to the service? How do employees decide that a counselling service has a value before they begin to use it? Hopefully, after they use it the value will be apparent. But a free service does not necessarily mean that it is used because it is valued. The large differences in the utilization figures reported by McLeod (2001: 58) may also suggest that there are other factors that dictate use other than because the counselling is being offered for free. The annual utilization figures varied between 1.4 percent to 20 percent of the employee populations in 18 companies. Other factors influence the take-up of counselling services.

EAP professionals take different stances on this issue; one clinical director believes that EAPs have a socio-political role and employees should not have to pay for these services. As companies push employees to be productive and consequently 'burn them out' the employee should not have to pay for the care they require as a result. This director believes that employees should use their EAPs as much as possible to get something else back from the company that demands so much of them. He points to comparative 'Did Not Attend' (DNA) rates between NHS counselling services and EAP counselling services. The DNA rates for his EAP company are approximately half of that for NHS services – yet both are free to the clients using them. The difference is in the motivation to use the services. This is crucial and indicates how important preparation, information and correct assessment is for helping employees access counselling services.

Another view from an experienced workplace counsellor adds to this debate. 'People feel that they owe me something'. This is because there is no immediate, tangible method for recognizing or rewarding the counsellor for what he or she has done. This counsellor is regularly offered gifts as 'thanks' from employees in one particular company. If employees feel that they owe something to a counsellor then this can affect the counsellor–client relationship at many levels. The presence of a fee may alleviate this difficulty, although it does not eliminate the problem.

The absence of fees was acknowledged by another counsellor-manager offering a free service to NHS employees. She observed that absence of fees definitely has an impact upon the service as 'people can mess you around'. They do not perceive the service as serious, credible or demanding any commitment from them. To address this she puts much effort into ensuring that the first session with an employee-client grab their attention and interest. It has to engage them and help them feel that they want to return for another session. This means that this counsellor works harder at establishing a positive rapport as quickly as possible with the employees. She describes this as harder than her work in private practice as she is searching to establish a value for the counselling with the employee in the first session.

Without the guidance of a fee, the employee-client may look for other ways of valuing the sessions, such as wondering how many other employees are waiting for the service, and comparing themselves favourably because they are having sessions while other employees are not. The employee may value having access to a scarce resource, and being given something that colleagues may not know about, care about or understand. This may help some employees feel 'special', lucky or different, and while this is positive it can also have other associations and pitfalls. The transference relation between counsellor and employee can be deepened by factors that may not be useful in the context of a brief therapy contract. For example, a client in a workplace setting was expressing her anxieties about the number of counselling sessions she had, and the prospect of using all her 'allotted number of sessions all at once'. This may have been an anxiety about what she was discovering about herself during the counselling process. However, she was also referring to using a precious resource and she made a reference to other employees whom she might be preventing from accessing the counselling because she was taking up the counsellor's time. This is not a new phenomenon and is a common anxiety that counsellors experience in other settings. But there is a reality about this in the workplace – there *is* a finite number of sessions per employee, the counsellor does have a limited amount of time and, in seeing one client, this means that the client's colleagues cannot yet be seen. In this case the client's dilemma had a direct link to her early life – she had a very uncertain position in her original family and apparently was constantly reminded to consider the welfare of her siblings and parents before herself.

As well as the projections of the employee, some counsellors may have anxieties about seeing a client without having a direct fee paid to them. This raises the issue of 'third party' payments: that someone

else pays for the sessions. Counsellors respond to 'third party' payments differently. Some counsellors may unconsciously try to add
value to the sessions. For example, a counsellor who becomes ideal-
ized may have unwittingly given an impression that the client is
'lucky' to be having such a good opportunity for free. But some counsellors idealize the employees they have as clients. This can occur in
some EAP settings where counsellors are recruited as affiliates and
work as part of a larger network. Depending on the size of the EAP
client population, and the number of affiliate counsellors in a geographical area, some affiliates may only receive a small number of
employee-clients each year. One EAP supervisor has noted that some
counsellors became unusually attached to these rather special clients,
because they rarely see EAP clients and want to give a good impression to the client, whose feedback to the EAP on the counselling is
felt to be significant. The counsellor may be anxious to maintain the
link with the EAP for financial reasons and because the counsellor
wants to continue on an EAP affiliate list. This supervisor suggests
that where an affiliate network is used rather than full-time counsellors, it is better to have a smaller number of counsellors seeing a
larger number of clients than the other way around. This also
increases the commitment of some counsellors to an EAP, and makes
the work with the employee-clients more ordinary. The need on the
part of counsellors to impress an EAP is less likely to prejudice the
work.

Some organizations have an arrangement with an external counselling service so that the organization may state that they provide a
counselling service for their employees, but the employees pay for
their own therapy. This may well raise issues if the employees,
imagining that they are getting something free, find they then have
to pay. The financial arrangement is obviously something the counsellor makes clear at the outset but, unless it has been made clear by
the employer before the first appointment, this is likely to lead to
some negative feelings, felt not just towards the organization, but
towards the counsellor as well.

Another issue that can arise is the limit set on the number of sessions that an employer agrees to pay for. For example, in one institution an employee referred himself for counselling, and was entitled
through the counselling contract, to have six free sessions with an
experienced workplace counsellor. Towards the end of the assessment session as the counsellor was repeating what had been agreed
as an appropriate focus for their work together, the employee-client
angrily asked why he was only allowed six sessions and why he could
not have more than the six, as he felt his problems deserved more

than that. The counsellor encouraged him to talk further about this, and the client said that the company had caused his problems and so they should provide an adequate source of solution and understanding. As the counsellor wondered how to reply, the client continued, becoming increasingly agitated and furious, blaming the company and his manager for his situation. He included the counsellor in a list that ran through the management, the personnel department and the chief executive, none of whom he felt were giving him what he needed. The counsellor felt that it would be unwise to defend the company that was being attacked, and was reluctant to get into any discussion about the number of counselling sessions available to employees. But the vehemence with which the client made the complaint enabled the counsellor to understand just how much the employee felt the company had imposed on him, and at this stage at least, how determined he was to blame the company rather than look at where his own responsibility lay.

Another example of the confusion that can occur is when an organization offers a limited number of free counselling sessions to employees through an external contractor: each employee is entitled to a maximum of, for example, ten free sessions. After the ten sessions, does the counsellor offer further counselling sessions to employees for a fee? In one organization some employees were being offered further sessions and others were not, and the fees varied with each counsellor. The organization felt that employees were being exploited. The understanding that the organization thought they had with the contractor was for time-limited brief therapy, free and open to all employees. Some EAPs make it clear to the counsellors they use that if a client wants more counselling it should not be with the same counsellor, but after consultation with the EAP, through referral to another counsellor. This obviates some of the risk of exploitation of positive feelings towards the counsellor.

Greenson (1967: 256) notices a 'defensive transference' that occurs among several types of patient and includes 'clinic cases treated without fee'. This transference has to be carefully exposed and shown up for what it is before any further treatment can take place. Usually in workplace counselling settings, such defences cannot be examined in much depth because of time constraints, the inappropriateness of in-depth work in a brief therapy environment, the reluctance of the clients to examine unconscious transferences and lack of training of workplace counsellors to do this form of analysis. However, these reasons do not mean that such defences do not exist and in some situations, it is possible to examine these issues briefly with a client in a workplace setting.

For example, an employee-client asked for clarification about the number of sessions 'due to me'. The number of sessions, in this case 12, had been discussed by the counsellor at the beginning of the brief therapy. The counsellor asked the employee what she meant by the phrase 'due to me'. She said she believed she had an 'entitlement' to a number of sessions, and she wanted to make sure that she got what she 'had a right to'. The counsellor felt the tone of this communication was aggressive and demanding, and that she was being attacked for withholding something that the employee believed was owed to her, not just by the employer, but also by the counsellor. The counsellor was able to look at the meaning of this with the client, linking it to other issues the employee was struggling with.

These different examples are reminders of the possible perceptions of a 'free service'. The way the service is advertised, or the popular perceptions about the service, might lead some employees to believe that counselling is a service they should expect. It is part of a 'bargain', a deal between management and staff, and like any other service/benefit that the employer offers, can be taken up and aggressively used by some clients. As counsellors enter a workplace to provide counselling, they rarely enter as a neutral agent. Indeed, the question of their identity is worth exploring further.

THE ACCLIMATIZATION PROCESS

Counsellors have to make several important adjustments to their counselling values, practice and objectives when they join a workplace counselling service. To call this 'acclimatization' is to recognize that a significant physical and psychological adaptation might need to be made to work in such an environment. For example, joining a local authority with a workforce of 18,000 employees after working as a primary care counsellor in a small, close-knit rural surgery with eight doctors and their staff can represent a huge adjustment. The counsellor has to find a way of 'fitting in'. Finding an entry point into a large anonymous group can be quite a problem. Adapting to the milieu of a company requires alertness, a clear sense of identity and patience. This is a distinctive feature of workplace counselling. Butler (1999) describes some of the expectations encountered by a workplace counsellor:

> They may be expected to help clients in a single session, to work with those who are not psychologically minded, to develop media other than one-to-one counselling, and to find ways of

disseminating their skills to empower others to whom clients more naturally turn for help. This represents a series of exciting opportunities, but requires a willingness to step outside the conventional framework of counselling.

(Butler 1999: 228)

A counsellor who works independently or in other settings does not have to adapt to the environment in quite the same way. It is comparable to a stranger becoming a member of an established family. At first, the family may be suspicious, curious or threatened by the presence of a newcomer. There could be territorial disputes if the newcomer sits in the wrong chair, envy and jealousy may be aroused if existing relationships are disturbed, and competition may develop for power and domination of the family. Alliances may be developed, renewed or broken as the newcomer finds a position in the family, if he or she is allowed to stay. The family too has to find a way of adapting and changing to allow the stranger in. All of these things happen when a workplace counsellor joins a company. Employees will 'check him or her out', he or she may be tested, looked at and examined. Simultaneously, the counsellor will be making initial impressions about the physical and psychological climate, which can remain as vivid and powerful memories.

The new counsellor has to learn the rules of the company, both official and unofficial versions. In many organizations, new employees are inducted and introduced to the systems and personnel that are significant, although in some organizations induction may be limited to being shown where the tea-making facilities and photocopier are. At one London teaching hospital, new counsellors are taken around the sites and formally and informally introduced to staff and all the services by the head of the counselling team. This is an ideal entry for a counsellor – a guided, careful entry. Being shown around also helps to make the counsellor visible. But induction may also mean that a counsellor picks up a sense of values in a company which run counter to her or his own values – counselling, after all, tends towards the more liberal, humanistic end of the scale, and does not necessarily sit easily with the assumptions of some businesses, where 'dog eats dog', profit is all and the employees are not given the respect that either they or the counsellor believe they should have. Another part of the acclimatization process involves the recognition by a new workplace counsellor of what it is necessary to know in order to function relevantly in the employing organization. This may mean information which counsellors do not usually have to have at their fingertips. A similar situation arises for a counsellor who works in an NHS GP surgery, who needs to have some idea about how the GPs and other professionals work with patients, although the counsellor is probably not medically trained. In the workplace setting there are many more procedures and practices that a counsellor will need to be aware of, because employee-clients will be discussing such issues. The counsellor needs to have an understanding of some of the working practices in order to distinguish real issues.

For example, an employee was talking to a counsellor about a formal 'grievance' he had taken out against his line manager. The client was very distressed and anxious about the deterioriating relationship with his manager and was expecting that the company grievance policy would quickly provide him with the support and resolution that he wanted. The counsellor had become familiar with the policy as she had listened to many other employees voicing similar expectations. After reading the policy and listening to employees as they endured this long and complex grievance process, she had an awareness of the company that the employee did not have, or did not want to have. The counsellor did not directly talk about the employee's excessive expectations but was able carefully to challenge some of the assumptions and hopes that the employee had brought to the sessions. With her company knowledge, she was able to 'keep an eye on the external reality of the situation'. Knowledge of grievance procedures had not in fact been included in this counsellor's basic training, but it was an important part of her new knowledge base when working for the company. Counsellors are sometimes offered places on internal training programmes – such as on management procedures and policies or trade union/staff association training sessions. Discussing these issues with an employee may not be an integral part of a counsellor's function, but it can be essential background knowledge.

In some organizations, counsellors have more than a counselling role. For example, in some large internal EAPs and counselling services counsellors provide training, mentoring, coaching, team development and so on. Therefore, it is important for them to know what is happening to the organization as a whole because they may have to discuss non-counselling issues with employees. For example, one internal EAP counsellor had a role that included mentoring for headteachers. She used many counselling skills in her work with headteachers, but she was on one occasion required to help a headteacher with a difficult relationship with the deputy head. This eventually involved discussing the local education authority's 'competency process' and how the head would handle it. The counsellor clearly needed to know what the process involved, how long each stage would take and how to assist the headteacher. To do this she had to discuss the process with a personnel expert, obtain and read the competency manual, understand it and then discuss it with the headteacher. It was a long way from her psychodynamic training! Such multiple roles in workplace counselling are common. Often counselling is situated in employee welfare units/departments where there are a variety of roles and functions.

Other issues that a counsellor may need to have a knowledge of include government legislation, current legal provisions and current trends in management practice. They need to be aware of issues such as bullying and harassment, equal opportunities, selection procedures, alcohol and drugs policies, flexi-time/time off in lieu, trade union representation, professional organizations, return to work interviews, sickness leave, compassionate leave, grievance procedures, mediation services, access to training for employees, management style/training and development programmes for employees, as well as how to access other services such Money Advice, Citizens Advice Bureaux, employment solicitors and so on. This list is a reflection of everything that can happen at work and everything that employees can bring to the workplace counsellor. Any of the related issues can have an impact on a counselling session and although a counsellor does not need to be an expert in any of these areas, awareness of how the issues affect employees is important.

CONCLUSION

As a counsellor enters the workplace setting and begins to become acclimatized to a particular group of clients and their working environment, new relationships within the organization begin to develop. The nature of these relationships can be fascinating and puzzling. They develop not just in counselling sessions, in case management or in meetings with personnel, but in corridors, by the photocopier and the drinks machine, as well as in committees and even the boardroom. Chapter 5 explores these important relationships, which, depending on how well they are handled, can make or undermine the workplace counselling service.

· FIVE ·

Professional relationships in counselling in the workplace

I tell you, I would rather be a swineherd, understood by the swine, than a poet misunderstood by men.

(Kierkegaard 1959: 19)

It is important for a workplace counsellor to determine whom he or she identifies with in an organization and to try to understand who identifies with them. In one company a workplace counsellor was experiencing the same dilemmas about allegiance, identity and loyalty as Kierkegaard's swineherd. This counsellor explained that the alliances that were important to him and his service were not necessarily the obvious ones that are essential to the success of a service. His loyalty was with the employee-clients, line managers, personnel officers, trade union officials, occupational health professionals, headteachers and unit managers who all worked in the organization with him and for him. He gave his services discreetly, professionally and 'in context' – that is, he knew the boundaries and ways to communicate about referrals, disputes and problems with employees. In return, although he did not consciously ask for it, he gained loyalty and respect from those he worked with. His community of support did not, however, include the senior management of the organization. He described the lip-service approach of senior managers, who usually excluded themselves from the services offered and excluded themselves from any responsibility for issues within the organization; responsibility for problems was passed so far up the hierarchy that it eventually disappeared and as it disappeared so did the prospect of any answers to the problems. Senior management did not want to understand what he did, were indifferent to his reports and 'spoke a different language'.

In this organization, senior management may have taken a defensive attitude to the workplace counselling service by excluding themselves from it, but this was not damaging to the service. The success of the counselling service was maintained by other employees. It did not require senior management backing – indeed such backing may have been harmful to the credibility of the service, according to the workplace counsellor. This counsellor was understood by the employees he helped – the swineherd was happy among his community. This is a factor in how an organization adopts an EAP, as noted by Sonnenstuhl and Trice: 'While top management support for the EAP may be essential to policy adoption, it is by no means sufficient for program implementation' (1995: 15).

Unfortunately, the important issue of a counsellor's working relationship with other employees within organizations who are not employee-clients has received very little attention from counselling research and writing. It is unfortunate because the position of workplace counsellors in organizations is fraught with all manner of complex boundary issues, operational and ethical problems, and relationship dynamics with other employees. In one sense, there is never a dull moment in a workplace counsellor's working life – there are always fresh, rich, psychological dilemmas to try to grapple with and understand. Early on in the career of a workplace counsellor, the counsellor has to try and make a decision about where he or she wishes to be within the organization. This can be a crucial decision and one that may need revisiting and redefining throughout his or her time in the organization. Is the counsellor on one side or another of the great divide of power, loyalty and allegiance in the workplace? Management, non-management or neither? Whatever the counsellor decides, this may well be reformulated for the counsellor by the employees, whether managerial and non-managerial, consciously and unconsciously. Workplace counsellors try to be independent, impartial, objective and professional. However, the *role* is not. The role is determined by the organization as well as the counsellor. This is another of the major differences for someone who has been working in a different setting, when starting a new phase of career as a workplace counsellor.

I believe that counsellors may have a certain fixed life span within an organization and then they move into something else through promotion or demotion, through change of interest or when they finish their useful life in one organization and leave to find another. The sort of creature that a counsellor could be compared to is not straightforward. Working within organizations can feel like a struggling octopus where each of the eight arms grapples with a different problem. In order to cope with the different demands the workplace counsellor needs to have eight powerful arms, each with different skills, suckers and muscles. He or she is not just a counsellor but has to be many things to many people in the organization. Like an octopus, the workplace counsellor has to be well camouflaged, observant and quick to react. However, an octopus may be a creature to be feared and so this may not be an entirely accurate comparison with a counsellor – although some employees may fear a counsellor! Then there are the major relational problems that workplace counsellors face every day of their working lives.

A counsellor who is sited in the workplace may want to be invisible, but sometimes the more employees they help in an organization, the more recognizable they become. Identity and recognition are not always useful for a workplace counsellor or for the employees they work with. The counsellor's discretion may become compromised by his or her visibility; a simple walk to the drinks dispenser can become a psychological obstacle course as he or she tries to avoid identifying certain employees by not acknowledging them, and to maintain relations with other employees they do not know by acknowledging them! Who does the counsellor acknowledge and how is it perceived in the public areas outside of the consulting room? The discretion of the counsellor is an interesting dilemma: in some situations the counsellor may be required to have a high profile and to be very visible and present – for example, by making a speech at a conference. In other situations, in other meetings, the counsellor may prefer to keep a very low profile, for example, when attending a meeting with a chief executive: entering and leaving the chief executive's office may need some thinking about, especially if the office is highly visible.

The problem of visibility can be seen in the following questions, which many counsellors employed within an organization will find themselves asking: with whom does the counsellor sit with at break time? Or eat with at lunch time? Is the counsellor included in some of the office rituals such as birthday celebrations, festive meals and events, the office party? Who is the counsellor 'close' to in the organization – does he or she have friends at work, outside the counselling service (as many other employees are likely to have)? What happens if the counsellor dislikes someone in the organization? How is this dealt with? What happens if the workplace counsellor is involved in a work issue or conflict as an employee in their own right?

An interesting example of a counsellor's nightmare is seen in this example of a relatively new counsellor working in an NHS employee counselling service. She decided to attend an internal course on the breakthrough technique that was being provided for all employees and was important in some employees' working situations. The counsellor felt like she stuck out in the training event like a 'sore thumb'. She felt very inhibited and unable to be herself on the course because other employees were very curious about her when she was introduced as an employee counsellor. Not only were they curious, but some were also quite disparaging, patronizing and confused about her status within the organization. The confusion also extended to the trainers, who somehow wanted her to be on a par with them – they included her in their references to themselves, as distinct from and separate to the other employees in the room. The counsellor became even more uncomfortable when a course participant started to tell her about her partner's job as a psychologist and proceeded to ask the counsellor about her own research techniques. Some of the other employees mocked her when it came to a physical exercise in the training with the comment, 'Oh well, if she can lift someone up, anyone can!' The counsellor had tried to be careful about how much she revealed about herself at the beginning of the course, as she had a sense of both being an employee like everyone else, and being set apart in some way and therefore not like everyone else. She was also unsure how much to reveal about herself in case one of the participants came to her as a client in the future. But her attempts to set boundaries were futile and she left the course with uncertain feelings about her role, the organization and to some degree herself. As a person-centred counsellor she was disappointed because of the huge incongruence she had experienced in the situation, not necessarily because of who the individuals were but because of the role she was in. The event raised serious questions for her and she decided that she would not take part in any further internal training nor deliver any, and would maintain the part-time status she then had at the counselling service rather than taking on the full-time employee status she had been offered.

RELATIONSHIPS BETWEEN A WORKPLACE COUNSELLOR AND OTHER EMPLOYEES

Workplace counsellors usually have relationships with many other employees, not just employees who are clients, or 'employee-clients'. Workplace counsellors have to have relationships with those who make referrals such as managers, personnel officers, trade union officials and so on. They usually have relationships with a peer group and with their own line manager. Each of these relationships requires understanding and examination.

As well as being a counsellor, the counsellor is an ordinary employee who may wish to have ordinary communications and relations at work like anyone else. Some internal workplace counsellors are perceived by employees as 'part of the furniture'; others are not known by other employees at all. Both situations have advantages and pitfalls and may have an impact on how the service is used and abused by employees. Workplace counsellors used by EAPs do not face such issues, as they do not usually use consulting rooms inside the organization and are 'external' in all senses. Their role is designed to be outside of the workplace and such difficulties rarely arise for them.

Workplace counsellors therefore have to recognize and acknowledge their relations with other employees at all levels. They have contracts with the employee-clients, the organization and their clinical supervisor. Tudor (1997) writes about the 'complexity of contracts' and uses a transactional analysis model to describe the contract that a counsellor may have with a client and organization as a simple triangular figure. It is useful as a visual description of the distance between client, counsellor and the organization. However, I believe the triangle could be developed to place the client – employee and workplace counsellor inside a circle that represents the organization, with the counsellor's corner of the triangle being nearest to the circumference of the organizational boundary, and in some circumstances such as an external EAP, the counsellor's corner of the triangle could extend beyond the organizational boundary (see Figure 5.1).

Carroll (1996: 17) represents these workplace counselling relationships with similar diagrams, and there are further variations that may be constructed, such as the relationship of the organization to the

Figure 5.1 A visual description of the distance between client-employee, counsellor and organization, within the organization

society or community it is situated within, as well as the various possibilities of relationships with clinical supervisors and professional bodies, and the socioeconomic-legal relationships that exist with other organizations such as local and central government and so on. Figure 5.1 illustrates the counsellor's position on the boundary of the organization and the world outside that organization. This is a crucial position but is not always permanent or fixed. It specifically describes the position of a salaried counsellor who is an employee of the organization, for example, an internal or 'in-house' counsellor. If the counsellor is contracted on a self-employed or freelance basis, the counsellor is outside the boundary that defines the limits of the organization. If the counsellor is contracted by an EAP their position is also outside the organizational circumference. The position is not always that close to the edge of the circumference, although the counsellor may be drawn nearer to the centre in some situations. For example, when a line manager asks the counsellor if an employee has attended counselling sessions – a common occurrence in many organizations (Sonnenstuhl 1986: 117) – the counsellor is being used as an internal management tool, and their position moves towards the centre of the organization, away from the employee-client relationship and the external boundary. If the counsellor remains firm with their own parameters, as is strongly suggested by Langs (1998), then the counsellor can maintain their position on the circumference.

Workplace counsellors are often unconsciously lured out of their role by other employees. Hirschorn describes what may happen when employees step out of their work role:

> First, anxiety about work can lead people to step out of their work roles. In this way, they turn away from work realities and create a surreal world in which challenges can be met with fantasies of omnipotence, dependence, or defensive denial. Second, when people depend on one another to do effective work, when they must collaborate, one person's anxiety may trigger an *anxiety chain* through which people deploy collective fantasies to deny risks. Third, these fantasies are filled with violence, as people both punish themselves for their own failings and imagine that others are their persecutors. Fourth, as people step out of role, they also step away from one another. They experience real others as though the others embodied the character-istics of fantasy figures, particularly fragmented or caricatured figures who are either all good and beautiful or all bad and evil.
> (Hirschorn 2000: 42)

Workplace counsellors are subject to these difficulties as much as any other employee. As a counsellor is encouraged to leave their role and come into the organization, away from the periphery, the 'anxiety chain' thickens and tightens around the counsellor and the employees involved. This influences referrals – what may seem to be an ordinary everyday occurrence can be fraught with complexities and the 'anxiety chain' can become tightly knotted and almost impossible to undo.

Carroll (1996: 18) refers to other positions that a counsellor may take up as part of their role: working with employees in denial that the organization exists; as allies to the organization; as allies to employees against the organization; and working between organization and employees. These positions can arise because the workplace counsellor is unclear about their role and so can be unconsciously manipulated into a different role, as Hirschorn suggests (2000: 42). Other forms of denial used defensively by a counsellor include denying the existence and importance of the clinical supervisor, the EAP, the counsellor-manager, the case manager and the employee's manager and colleagues. The counsellor may bring their own personal values into the sessions such as that work is meaningless, that there is no life outside of work or that only certain occupations have value and so on. These may seem extreme positions, but they can occur since roles in organizations are subject to powerful unconscious projections and fantasies, and counsellors are exposed to them as much as any other employee.

A 'HEADS DOWN' CULTURE

The workplace counsellor is part of a system and sometimes the counsellor can have a very direct impact upon the culture. Workplace counsellors fulfil a number of roles and responsibilities. For example, a psychodynamic counsellor working in a public sector organization worked beyond the boundaries of regular counselling and contributed in other ways to the organization that employed him. This counsellor steadily adhered to the ordinary daily boundaries of the work with individual employees. However, occasionally, as he became known through the feedback of employees at all levels in the management structure, he was asked to contribute to public conferences and events that focused on stress in the organization. Initially he was reluctant to raise his profile in such a manner, but he strongly believed in getting the message across to employees that there was help available to them if they needed it, that it was provided within the organization as well as externally by a counselling company. But as his profile developed he began to see that there was (and had been for many years) a 'heads down' culture that thrived in the organization. This 'heads down' culture was primarily based upon an anxious fantasy of what would happen to employees if they dared to raise their heads 'above the parapet' and talk about what was happening in their teams, groups, departments and working lives. Often the counsellor heard phrases such as 'I don't want to rock the boat', or 'It is better to not to stick your neck out in this unit'. He heard this so often that he began to observe patterns and themes in the daily working experiences of these employees.

This 'heads down' culture was due to a number of factors and had become a defence mechanism that served a useful purpose for the employees. Some of the main factors that were identified included bullying and harassment from colleagues and line managers, shortage of front-line resources, confusion and lack of direction about the future of the organization, 'change for change's sake' and lack of training and career development opportunities. The workplace counsellor was intrigued by the predominant and pervasive management style. He recognized that there were many committed and courageous managers who were respected by their subordinates who continued, despite real problems, to deliver high-quality, useful services to the public and to other employees. However, the pervasive style fitted into some concepts described in Gabriel's *Organizations in Depth* (1999), specifically Hirschorn's chapter on leaders and followers. Narcissistic and heroic leadership styles were dominant in the managerial hierachy. As he discussed these issues in different forums in the organization, employees commented on his courage in voicing these ideas. He was asked to repeat these discussions in other parts of the organization and he developed a mediation system in line with the existing bullying and harassment policy. He was provided with a small team of volunteer employees to help him whose initial training comprised a conflict resolution model, as delivered by the Tavistock Consultancy Services. Conflict resolution could then be actively used to resolve inter-employee disputes, before a formal process was necessary. He recognized that the culture would take years to change, but he also knew he had played a significant part in starting the process.

THE DYNAMICS OF REFERRAL

Referral usually means one person passing another to a third party for help, assistance, specialist treatment or some other care that the third party provides. For example, in the workplace a manager may refer an employee to the workplace counsellor for counselling. They are passing the employee over to the care of an individual who has been contracted for their skills, experience and training as a counsellor. The counsellor receives the referral, contact with the employee is established and the process begins. Methods of referral vary from written proforma sheets or other elaborate systems that are used in some organizations to simple telephone conversations, discussions in corridors and emails, that prompt a counselling process for an employee. The referral system usually reflects something important about communication within an organization. But this is not always obvious – for example, in one public sector organization referrals to the in-house counsellor are not bureaucratic but very informal. This reflects some of the anxiety employees feel about the discretion and confidentiality of written information. A discreet telephone call to the in-house service is the preferred method of self-referral or third party referral.

The communication chosen for the initial contact with a workplace counselling service, and other aspects of the referral, reveal some of the conscious and unconscious features of the organization, employees and the workplace counselling service. Transference, counter-transference, projection, projective identification and many other defence mechanisms are present. Some of these defences can be seen in the material, even in short-term counselling sessions. The referral process is part of Hirschorn's 'anxiety chain' – an employee or manager passes anxiety on to the counsellor to manage. The counsellor contains and manages some of this anxiety, and passes some of it on to their clinical supervisor, and so passes some the anxiety out of the organization, unless the supervisor is also part of the organization, which is very rare in the United Kingdom. The counsellor acts like a waste pipe for an organization. The pipe may have some sophisticated filters and even two-way valves, but essentially it is a conduit for anxiety waste products.

Sonnenstuhl suggests that employees who self-refer:

experience two social consequences. First, they feel stigmatized by their involvement in the program, and this perception prompts them to conceal their involvement from others. Second, by complying with the psychotherapist's instructions, they experience a secondary gain that allows them to recontain their problems within the contexts of their family and work lives.

(1986: 151)

Self-referral usually happens when an employee approaches a workplace counselling service by telephone or email. The service arranges an assessment appointment with a workplace counsellor and the process begins. Alternatively, a third party may contact the service and ask for an employee to be contacted, and an agreement will be made about how much feedback will be supplied to the manager. The third party could be a manager, a personnel officer, an occupational health professional or a trade union official.

The EAPA UK provides standards for referral:

> Managerial referrals are an addition to other managerial interventions and actions. They are appropriate when a manager is faced with an employee where there is clear evidence of deteriorating and unacceptable work performance. The matter is no longer one where a manager might nudge or 'informally' refer an employee to the EAP but one where the manager has a responsibility for work performance or behaviour and must intervene proactively and skilfully.

(2000: 91)

As the EAPA suggests, referral needs to be handled carefully so that the employee is not coerced into counselling. However, self-referral is usually the main source of workplace counselling services and the usual route into counselling for most employees who use it. But what does self- or third-party referral mean for workplace counsellors? Most counselling literature contains advice on how to refer clients to other agencies, professionals and services, but there is not much attention paid to what it means to receive such a referral. Lago and Kitchin (1998: 76) refer to 'reception and threshold' processes that help a person become a client, and Mander (2000: 106) describes some of the difficulties that arise when a client is referred to another service. But what about the relationship that exists between referrer and the person receiving it? It may only be a brief and distant relationship, however, both parties are connected by the client and the connection may have an influence on the counselling. For example, a manager was asked for a discreet discussion with a workplace counsellor about a member of her team. The manager revealed her concerns about the mental health of the employee and did not know what to do. The workplace counsellor heard this worry and offered his services for the manager to make a third party referral.

Agreement was reached about levels of disclosure, which the counsellor would discuss with the employee. Then the counsellor contacted the employee and discussed boundaries of confidentiality after the manager had told the employee about her discussion with the counsellor. The counsellor made an assessment appointment and during the assessment session discussed the possibility of a psychiatric referral with the employee. The employee gave consent to the counsellor to discuss this with the manager; the employee went to see her doctor and an appointment was quickly arranged for a psychiatric assessment. Later the manager told the counsellor that the employee had been given a temporary diagnosis of paranoid schizophrenia and the employee was having the necessary treatment. This is a good example of how several levels of referral are sometimes necessary yet can work smoothly and efficiently. Sensitive handling of the issue was crucial for all the parties involved – the manager, the employee-client and the counsellor.

A less happy relationship can be seen in the following example, where a personnel officer, one of the EAP manager's peers in the organization, asked if a particular employee had been in contact with the EAP manager for counselling. This employee apparently was threatening to sue the organization for lack of care and assistance throughout a prolonged work-based crisis. The EAP manager was firm about her boundaries and politely told the personnel officer that she could not divulge such information because of the code of ethics that she was bound to as a BACP-accredited counsellor. The relationship with the personnel officer detioriated and she told the EAP manager that she could no longer use some of the facilities that the EAP manager had been using. To the EAP manager this felt like a 'tit for tat' that had resulted from her sticking to her boundary of confidentiality with the client.

This is an example of a common difficulty in relations to workplace peers and is a reminder that some peers assume that they have access to privileged information. Gray (1994: 68) recognizes these problems and suggests

> Usually, I have found a comment such as 'I hope this doesn't seem unhelpful' allows other workers to talk about their own belief in the importance of privacy. None the less, it must be added that there are times when all our skill and tact does not result in a good outcome. We are sometimes seen as unhelpful, obtuse and unnecessarily secretive.

Paproski and Haverkamp (2000) outline some of the problems that prevent effective referrals to and from counsellors and other professionals, stating that there is common agreement that 'inter-disciplinary collaboration among professionals provides competent and effective care for the client. Even so, there are no explicit guidelines on how to conduct interdisciplinary communication and collaboration' (2000: 85).

The problems they identify in the referral of a client from a counsellor to other mental health workers include (2000: 87):

1 client protection;
2 variation in training and professionalism;
3 time constraints;
4 reluctance;
5 lack of knowledge and awareness;
6 lack of coordination and case management.

The problem of 'reluctance' is crucial for a workplace counsellor to understand. Reluctance can be apparent at many levels, conscious and unconscious. For example, reluctance by third parties to refer an employee to the counselling service and reluctance of the employee to attend because they have been referred by a third party (both of which may illuminate the nature of their relationship), and reluctance of the counsellor to take the referral (for all manner of reasons such as exhaustion, complexity, boundary issues, waiting lists, annual leave and so on).

There may also be reluctance by the counsellor to refer an employee to other services or professionals. This important point is also identified by Paproski and Haverkamp (2000) and will be famil-iar to counsellors working in other settings – to whom does a counsel-lor refer a client? If a counsellor needs to refer a client for further mental health treatment or care there are real problems because of the huge shortage of professional services; or where they are avail-able, there is often a lengthy waiting list. In some areas of the United Kingdom it is not uncommon to wait up to one year for an appoint-ment at a psychotherapy clinic. If a client needs psychotherapy and is unable to pay for it privately, where is he or she to go to receive the care they require? Unfortunately, this can mean that some work-place counsellors 'hang on' to clients because they fear that there is no further help available – although holding on to clients in any setting can also be a counter-transference issue.

Reddy provides an example of a counsellor *not* referring a client on:

There are those who stick with a client through thick and thin to the point where they stray hopelessly beyond the boundaries of their competence, to say nothing of their comfort. One company

counsellor was suddenly told by her client that he was a transvestite. She had no idea how to deal with the situation, was even
somewhat confused between a transvestite and a homosexual.
She felt trapped because it had been said in confidence. But in
purely practical terms she was unable to be of much help, should
have said she was out of her depth and asked him if she might
refer him to another counsellor (equally in confidence) who was
more experienced.

(1998: 114)

The counsellor needs to be aware of the possibility of referring on
and to have sufficient knowledge of local resources if the need arises.
Other forms of help may be required such as legal, financial or career
advice and each of these may have a referral system. An example of
this comes from an internal EAP in a public sector organization: an
employee referred herself to the employee assistance service through
the internal email system. The service assistant returned the message
offering an assessment appointment. The employee had not identified any of the issues that she wished to speak about and the service
assistant had not asked what the issues were, as these would be discussed in the assessment session. At the end of the assessment session, the service assistant had identified the need for counselling and
for direct financial advice about money problems the employee had.
The employee was given the telephone number for the external
counselling service and the assistant encouraged the employee to
self-refer for counselling. The service assistant discussed referring the
employee to a local, free debt advice centre and in the session, with
the employee's agreement, the assistant telephoned the debt advice
centre, spoke to a debt adviser she knew and passed the telephone
over to the employee who then made an appointment with the debt
advisor. The employee was sent an evaluation form and was pleased
with the service from the service assistant. This service assistant was a
trained counsellor but unable to accept the referral for counselling
as she had a full counselling caseload and was working with the
maximum number of employee-clients that the service permitted.
Assessments like this are part of the service and could also be
described as 'referral sessions'.

Some referrals highlight the multiple relationships that workplace
counsellors and EAP workers have within and outside of the organizations that they serve. Malan's 'triangle of conflict' and 'triangle of
person' (2001: 90) can be applied to the dynamics of referral. The
'conflict' triangle features anxiety, defence and hidden feelings and
the 'person' triangle features parent, others and the transference to

the therapist. Hidden feelings directed towards the 'other' can be seen in hidden feelings directed towards the organization. This may take many forms, such as an employee's hatred directed towards his or her manager, erotic feelings directed towards co-workers, jealousy manifesting itself as competition between teams in an organization and so on. When a workplace counsellor receives a referral from a manager, the counsellor can become the 'other' in Malan's triangle and then may have to work at the employee–counsellor relationship to re-position herself or himself to receive the employee's hidden feelings in the transference. One example is when an employee has been referred by their manager and it becomes apparent in the counselling sessions that the employee is relating to the counsellor as if the counsellor were the manager. This can become extremely complicated and impossible to resolve if the transference is very negative and if there are only a limited number of sessions in which to address it. In such situations, the counsellor has to be more present, active and clear about their function with the employee, which in itself can help overcome some of the negative transference.

Receiving referrals involves accepting feelings that may belong in the relationship that the employee has with the referrer. When a manager refers an employee, they are to a degree also referring themselves. They are making a statement about the needs of the employee and about their inability to help. This is constructive when managers know that they are not counsellors. However, not all referrals are like this. Some managers refer employees punitively. Their expectation is that the employee will be fixed, cured, 'sorted out' or 'put straight'. They may be saying, 'Thank goodness, that I (the manager) don't have to try and deal with it'. The problem is passed on, and the manager can claim that he or she has carried out their duty by referring the 'problem' to the counsellor. There are still many organizations that try to use counselling as another management tool for correcting employees, or as a psychological waste bin. Counsellors who work in these organizations understandably receive all of the anxiety and anger that produces the referral in the first instance – since the employee has been sent out of the manager's anger, frustration, denial, impotence and so on. Any or all of these feelings can accompany the employee into the counselling room.

There are a number of relationships that a counsellor needs to establish and maintain in an organization, for example, with their line manager, immediate peer colleagues and team members, personnel officers, occupational health doctors and trade union officers. In some situations it is also useful to establish good working relationships with key secretaries, administrators, committee clerks, elected members and even shareholders. With large workforces extensive networking is impossible, although it is obviously easier in a small workforce, but the very size of a small organization can lead to problems: when perhaps employees are related to, married to or in relationships with other employees, and where boundaries about confidentiality, dual relationships and referrals can become quite confusing.

RELATIONSHIPS BETWEEN WORKPLACE
COUNSELLORS AND THEIR LINE MANAGERS

> Managers do two basic things: they manage processes and supervise people. Effective managers integrate the two in ways that increase productivity and improve the quality of work life.
> (Egan 1993: 66)

Not all workplace counsellors have 'managers', as they may be self-employed, used on a sessional basis by an organization or are freelance in some other way. However, some workplace counsellors do have line managers who are not necessarily counsellors themselves. Some line managers are qualified and experienced counsellors who have been promoted into managerial positions. Their contact with workplace counsellors varies from being relaxed to being anxiety-provoking. Some of the difficulties that arise can be attributed to the independent nature, and what might be described as professional awkwardness, of some counsellors.

One counsellor-manager describes managing counsellors as a difficult yet stimulating function. Working with a group of highly trained intuitive individuals can be an exhilarating experience. However, ordinary communication is sometimes much more complicated – for example a manager asked one of the counsellors to do something, but the counsellor believed that she was being offered a choice and that there were several options open to her. For the manager, there were no options – a task had to be completed and it was the counsellor's job to complete it. A debate with the manager followed, the task remained incomplete and the manager went to her own line manager with the problem. The counsellor's manager felt angry, ineffective and frustrated by the behaviour of the counsellor, and with her own lack of assertiveness.

Being 'managed' is a difficult and unpopular subject with some counsellors. Many counsellors do not want to be managed, preferring their own autonomy (a counselling watchword), controlling their own workload and being answerable only to the client and their supervisor. Some counsellors say that the work they do with individuals precludes them from any other organizational issues. They feel that their focus has to be exclusively the individual in front of them and that if their focus is distracted from the client then problems in the counselling relationship may follow.

I have some sympathy with this position as counsellors in the workplace can find themselves facing very complex dilemmas. Even in established workplace counselling services, some counsellors have difficulty accepting the authority of a manager, or even understanding the role of a manager; they seem unable to see their own roles as anything more than that of being a counsellor, even though they are part of an organization. This occurs whether or not the manager is a counsellor; indeed, sometimes managers who are counsellors may have an even more difficult task trying to manage other counsellors, and may find themselves trying to prove their counselling ability, knowledge and credibility.

The work milieu can be both judgemental and competitive – quite contrary to the climate that most counsellors look to work in. Nonetheless, they are subject to all of the vicissitudes, demands and pressures of an organization, like any other employee. Unfortunately some counsellors forget their own position in an organization because of their necessary focus on individuals and take on a role of 'saving' employees from the 'dreadful' organization, despite being themselves employees in that organization.

Lago and Kitchin (1998) address some of these issues and provide a guide to management theory and practice for counsellors. They write about useful management techniques, such as using personality questionnaires to recruit personnel who will fit the organization (1998: 116); and they recognize that counsellors, who are usually highly trained and sophisticated, may be a difficult group of staff to manage:

> Though deeply committed to personal learning, development and improvement, both for themselves and their clients, they may not be comfortable with the organizational and management demands of the counselling setting. Indeed, the counsellor may not appreciate the activities the manager engages in, in their management role. Mental health professionals may therefore prove to be a very complex group to manage!
>
> (Lago and Kitchin 1998: 114)

One of the reasons that some counsellors are difficult to manage is because they believe that the clients are their property, their responsibility, their work. This concept of ownership of clients is directly in conflict with many counselling theories and methods of working, but it is this conflict that gets acted out in many of the difficulties that can occur between workplace counsellors and their line managers. This occurs in EAPs as well, and one EAP has a clause in the affiliate contract that addresses this: '[****] EAP Limited is the referring agent and has full clinical responsibility for the client. It is therefore important that [****] EAP Limited be kept informed of any issues which may affect that responsibility' (internal document). The client temporarily belongs to the EAP not the counsellor. The EAP is contracted to the organization that employs the client. This reality is often ignored by many workplace counsellors, who treat the client as their property. Some counsellors believe that this ownership is not to be challenged or interfered with by any other, and this includes a line manager. Such defensive positions taken by some counsellors are reinforced by the use of the confidentiality clause – no one else is allowed into this relationship because the work is strictly confidential.

The difference between the private work in the consulting room is in stark contrast to the very public work done by the counsellor's manager, as Lago and Kitchin (1998: 129) point out: 'The public sphere in which management work is carried out is in direct contrast to the private arena of therapy'.

Lago and Kitchin (1998) outline the functions of a counselling service manager, particularly emphasizing the importance of the manager ensuring that adequate working conditions are available for the counsellors to enable them to do their work, which can be painful, demanding and emotionally exhausting. The manager acts as the provider of a containing environment for the counsellors, in a similar way that counsellors provide a containing relationship and environment for the employee-clients. This of course can lead to a variety of transferences and counter-transferences for both the managers and counsellors.

A good example of a containing environment is seen in one NHS trust. The counselling coordinator has a managerial role in the staff counselling service. She is a qualified and experienced workplace counsellor and oversees the work of several staff counsellors. When a new staff counsellor is recruited, the manager arranges a series of appointments for the new counsellor with a variety of employees, managerial and non-managerial, within the trust. This is part of an induction programme that the manager arranges and is an important introduction to the trust. The people whom the new counsellor sees are significant in many ways. Some appointments are jointly attended by the new counsellor and the coordinator, such as the introduction to the deputy director of nursing. Other appointments are arranged so that the counsellor can begin to develop his or her own sense of the organization; and the coordinator is keen for the counsellor to listen to employees who are not talking about problems or difficulties. This is to enable the counsellor to have the opportunity of seeing the organization from the angle of individual employees in normal work circumstances.

Another function of this induction is to help the new counsellor locate himself or herself within the organization. In this process, the new counsellor immediately becomes visible to the other employees and managers, who undoubtedly will be assessing him or her as he or she is also assessing employees and the organization.

An interesting question is whether managers of counsellors have to have undertaken counselling training. An equally interesting question is whether counselling training interferes with management practice. There are many courses that exist for managers to learn and practice counselling skills, but none for counsellors to become managers or to use management skills in their working lives, yet this seems a vital need as workplace counsellors proceed in their careers and become the managers of others.

To meet this situation I suggest that management training for counsellors who are managers, who have been promoted to a management position, or who find themselves having to manage other employees and counsellors would be helpful. As Egan asserts, managers 'are usually not neutral. They add either net value or cost' (1993: 10). Organizations with counselling services have reasons for the establishment of such services, ranging from rather obscure or ambiguous motives to clear profit protection motives. A good enough counsellor will add value to the organization. A good enough counsellor-manager will add value to the counselling team *and* to the employing organization.

A management course for counsellors should begin with the assumption that the workplace counsellor-manager adds value to the organization. It should include a combination of process skills, content skills, a systemic approach to managing and a module on the organizational applications of 'iceberg' skills.

Process skills

These include:

self awareness, managing personal stress, solving problems creatively, establishing supportive communication, gaining power and influence, improving employee performance through motivation, empowering employees, delegating and decision making, managing conflict, conducting effective group meetings, and team building

(Egan 1993: 15)

Content skills

These are the essential components of everyday effective management that serve the objectives of an organization (Egan 1993: 16):

- formulate, implement, and fine-tune strategy;
- stay in touch with the changing needs of customers;
- design effective and efficient work programmes;
- make sure that business-enhancing quality and customer service programmes are in place;
- establish cost-containment procedures;
- formulate and re-formulate the structure to make sure that it continues to serve the business;
- find new ways of making a reasonable structure work;
- establish jobs and roles with the kind of flexibility that serves the business;
- help design the kind of human resource management systems that help workers give their best efforts;
- find ways of making sure that well-designed human resource systems are effectively used by managers and supervisors;
- choose managers and supervisors because of their managerial and supervisory potential;
- help establish a management development process and make it work;
- develop and use the performance management system as a tool for increased productivity;
- develop strategic, operational, and human resource plans to make sure all the above happens;
- move institution-enhancing agendas through changing political currents within the organization;
- create and reinforce the kind of culture that serves the business;

- exercise leadership to achieve results beyond the ordinary, in all the above.

Some counsellor-managers may be daunted by such a huge list, but I have met several energetic and effective counsellor-managers who are fulfilling all of these requirements without realizing it and are still able to have a small counselling caseload. Egan's list does not have to be accomplished all at once. These daily tasks may be thought about or worked on gradually, but they involve long-term planning and commitment from the counsellor-manager and the organization. The measurement of counsellor performance will require an efficient system such as CORE to be used on a daily basis. As mentioned in Chapter 3, CORE demands management of counsellors. If CORE is only used to measure client benefit from counselling, then only half of its potential is being used.

Some counsellor-managers may ask what chance there is for any counselling with all these other tasks. Indeed, counselling may be restricted to a small number of clients, but the 'client' for a counsellor-manager is the organization.

A systemic approach

Managers need to have broad perspectives of the organization that go beyond their own technical experience and training. They need to have a sense of how their team fits in with other teams and how they are linked, integrated, contradictory, competitive and complementary to the whole. Decisions taken in one part of an organization usually have an effect on another part, since decisions are rarely isolated in their impact.

Egan describes a systemic approach as 'a template for doing things properly, a comprehensive process together with a common language' (1993: 17). He gives examples of companies that use quality control or marketing to establish a shared framework for all to follow and develop with each other. Egan's models in 'adding value' are interconnected and interdependent, all part of a whole system. Counsellor-managers need to learn about whole systems that incorporate 'strategy, customers' requirements, work design and flow, products and services, customer service, organizational structure, human resource management systems, coaching and counselling, system-wide leadership' (1993: 17).

Systems theory is not new to many counsellors, and the concept of integrating the different dynamics of the individual's internal world and life experience is a daily task. This is similar to helping an organization to meet objectives, incorporating all of the dilemmas, conflicts and defences that obstruct such integration. But applying these concepts to an organization and a team that a counsellor works within is new to many counsellors and counsellor-managers.

The application of 'iceberg' skills

When a counsellor-manager begins to use his or her authority to establish appropriate boundaries within a system the counsellor-manager becomes an 'object' in the system and this can become an extremely complex position. Thus training that helps counsellor-managers recognize and work with counter-transference is another essential element of the course.

Counter-transference is one of the many essential techniques and methods I refer to as 'iceberg' skills. This image is a simplification of the notion of what is conscious and what is unconscious in our lives, and is similar to the phrase 'under the surface' used by the Tavistock Consultancy Service to describe their function with individuals, teams and organizations. It is for me a short-hand description for transference, counter-transference, defence mechanisms, free association, interpretation and conscious and unconscious communication. While it is not essential for counsellor-managers to have undertaken psychodynamic training, some of these concepts are the most useful for further understanding of organizations and, in particular, the counsellor-manager's position.

Working with counter-transference involves the recognition and understanding of feelings and thoughts that may initially be unconscious; through a process of analysis, discussion and reflection the workplace counsellor can become aware of what they were experiencing at a given time with an employee, a manager or a team. Understanding what the counsellor is feeling can provide rich insight into what could be happening in the consultancy room, the corridor or the boardroom, between the counsellor and other employees. Just as counter-transference can be extremely valuable in the therapeutic process it also has relevance organizationally. The counsellor-manager needs to be aware of its importance and learn how and when to feed back such observations to the organization, and to which person in the organization to address the reservations so that the feedback is properly heard. Iceberg skills require careful and sensitive timing and sometimes clear and patient repetition, what we might call 'therapeutic diplomacy'. If knowledge of counter-transference is to be of any assistance to an organization, it has to be discussed in the relevant environment, with the right employees/managers, in a manner that will not alienate the counsellor-manager from the organization. The counsellor-manager may expect resistance and a variety of other defences, and if the point is too harshly made, the counsellor-manager may lose important relationships and connections.

Management training for counsellors might also include techniques to measure outcomes of workplace counselling and counselling performance, and skills in decision-making, designing work flow, negotiating staffing levels and understanding business tools such as sales, marketing and delivery.

WORKING RELATIONSHIPS FOR COUNSELLORS IN EAPs

Those who work for EAPs are in a very different position to counsellors who are integral to an organization. For a start, EAP counsellors are usually referred to as 'affiliates' or associates, one of a number in a network, who the EAP contact to provide counselling to employees in different geographical locations. The counsellors work for an EAP and are paid by the EAP but they are usually self-employed and may be affiliated to more than one EAP – an arrangement that meets the needs of the EAPs and the counsellors. It is a relationship of mutual dependence with the affiliate having limited control over the situation with the employee-client once the referral to the affiliate has been made; in other words, they are probably limited to providing a set number of sessions and have to refer the client back to the EAP if more counselling is required.

The affiliate sits between the employee-client, the EAP, the client-organization and the clinical supervisor; a complex position however neutral and otherwise independent the counsellor may be. Being an affiliate is an unusual position for many counsellors but the arrangement often works very successfully. Cooper and Highley-Marchington (1998: 55) report that counsellors 'were relatively satisfied on the whole, with carrying out EAP work'. McLeod (2001) cites other research that supports this finding, for example, Machin (1995) says '67% reported high levels of satisfaction with their EAP work' and Cunningham (1992) writes '71% were satisfied with EAP work, 26% were ambivalent'.

The Cooper and Highley-Marchington report provides some interesting figures that help to illuminate the working lives of EAP affiliates. For example, '65% did EAP counselling for less than 10 hours per week' (1998: 43); 'EAP counselling only accounted for about 10% of a professional counsellor's work' and 72% of 'counsellors performed their EAP work in their own home' (1998: 44). This last figure raised some concerns for the authors as 'providers had not inspected the homes of over 50% of the counsellors who used their own homes for EAP counselling' (1998: 44).

Another concern for many counsellors in this report highlights the absence of rigorous selection and recruitment of counsellors by EAP providers – some are recruited by a telephone call: '18% of counsellors had been selected without any form of interview, and a number had been hired solely on the recommendation of a third party' (1998: 47). However, these procedures vary among the EAPs and many counsellors feel adequately supported by the structure of the EAPs. Further training and a higher level of supervision were two areas where the authors found counsellors wanted more from the EAPs.

Not every counsellor is comfortable with the demands of being an affiliate. Cagney (1999) summarizes some of the important demarcations for an affiliate counsellor:

> Clinicians are traditionally trained to regard the relationship of the therapist and client as sacrosanct. As an EAP affiliate, they are working with an 'employee client'. The focus of their work together is to identify problem areas, explore possible solutions and engage in short-term problem resolution.
>
> The EAP professional has multiple constituencies including the supervisor, the employer organization, the EAP vendor, and at times even public safety. All the EAP constituencies have legitimate interests in the outcome of the case. This complex relationship has to be understood by both the affiliate and the client and managed by the EAP vendor.
>
> (1999: 68)

One EAP affiliate counsellor described the work as 'much more *managed* than a private practice', and even though most of the employee-clients self-refer, there is an understanding that the process will be scrutinized. This was accepted by the counsellor as she still had a large amount of autonomy in the work she did with the employee-client. Autonomy is an important value for the affiliate counsellor and as Sonnensthul (1986) points out there are four important elements that 'support their perception of autonomy: selectivity, alternative statuses, lack of close supervision, and enforcement of confidentiality' (1986: 113). The desire for an absence of close supervision seems to be contradictory to Cooper and Highley-Marchington's (1998) report suggesting that many counsellors were actively seeking more supervision provision from the EAPs.

However, Sonnenstuhl is referring to a desire to feel free to work to their abilities – 'give people freedom and they will perform' (1986: 115) – rather than for an absence of clinical supervision.

There are two questions that test the relationship between an affiliate EAP counsellor and the EAP provider: how does a counsellor report back to an organization on difficult or problematic organizational issues that may need attention? And does the affiliate have any organizational responsibility?

Regarding the first question, one affiliate who works for a number of EAPs reported that the larger EAP providers, such as ICAS, have been able to receive her comments about a company because they have close and successful relationships already established with the client companies. Smaller 'one man band' EAPs struggle with this because they have not thought through the process and implications of feeding difficult information back to a company. Another affiliate suggests that often the EAPs know about the problems within a company because they have taken time to explore the culture of a company and have been able to brief their counsellors before sending them a referral. When this has not been possible and a difficulty in a company has been identified by an employee-client to an affiliate then, with consent by the employee-client given to the EAP, it often appears that companies want to know about the difficulty and that the EAP can be both an important ear piece for and then a mouth piece to an organization.

The second question of organizational responsibility appears to be more difficult for some affiliates. One affiliate reported that in her private practice it is very clear that she has clinical responsibility. However, her organizational responsibility is not always clear with some EAP work. An employee-client who had been referred to this affiliate was unsuitable for counselling and needed psychiatric treatment. The affiliate wrote a referral letter to support this to the employee, their GP and the EAP. The EAP then passed this letter on to the company with the employee's consent. The affiliate felt slightly aggrieved at being sent an inappropriate client and wondered who had responsibility for the safety of the employee-client and the employee's colleagues. This scenario highlights a common counselling phenomenon – that some people are unsuitable for counselling – but also raises the issue of responsibility to and for the workplace. A different affiliate reported that she knows quite clearly that it is the EAP that has total responsibility for the employee-client, not the affiliate, because this is written in her contract with the EAP, which is itself a reflection of the contract that the EAP signs with the client-company. In some EAP work it is not so clear, not being addressed in any contract.

Many affiliates find that the workplace issues that employee-clients present are a means of helping the employee with other issues that are linked to workplace problems. For example, one affiliate used the problems that an employee had with an overbearing manager as a direct link to what the employee had told her about his early life with his father. Linking workplace issues to personal history and pathology is an everyday process for many affiliates, as much as it is for counsellors located in the workplace.

One affiliate describes how he hates being over-managed. 'I am an experienced therapist and I resent a case manger telling me what to do!' He gave an example of an EAP that had not clarified the role of case managers and so, sometimes, depending on which case manager he reported to, the case manager might try to offer clinical supervision, 'management' or information. This led to confusion and meant that participation in case management became a chore.

Reports from affiliates about their experiences working for EAPs are very illuminating. For example, one affiliate found that the staff at one EAP 'always sound very stressed and in a rush to do everything. This must rub off on the employee-clients if they are like that with them as well'. Another likes working for a small EAP because 'all the correspondence is personally signed, and the Director seems to be involved and interested in what is happening'. The EAP staff handle the employee-clients well, which is important for the referral process from employee to EAP and then to the affiliate. EAP staff are an essential part of the process whereby an employee-client reaches the affiliate. Undoubtedly unconscious messages for good or ill are picked up and transmitted through this process. If an employee is handled carefully and patiently by the EAP this can help the affiliate establish a successful working relationship.

Some affiliates, through experience, do not want to be associated with some EAPs or companies because of 'shoddy practices'. However, overall the affiliate–EAP relationship appears to be successful and productive for all involved.

THE RELATIONSHIP BETWEEN THE ORGANIZATION AND WORKPLACE COUNSELLOR

There is one final aspect, which has, in one way, run through this chapter, and that is that the counsellor is 'just' another employee, like any other person in the workplace, subject to the same difficulties as all other employees in the organization, affected by internal pressures within the organization as much as anyone else.

There are two main categories of pressure produced by the organization that workplace counsellors may encounter: contractual, pressure and whole-system dynamics.

The first pressure that may affect a workplace counsellor may be the negotiation of their contract. The financial and time constraints of the contract may be clear, fixed for a given length of time and explicit, or they may be vague or temporary for an unclear length of time. Either the ambiguity or clarity has the potential to become an uncomfortable pressure if other factors begin to arise. For example, a workplace counsellor on a permanent contract may begin to experience, consciously or unconsciously, pressure from employees facing redundancy, on temporary contracts or facing reduction in hours/ overtime etc. The employees may resent the perceived permanence of the counsellor as they face difficulties. They may believe that the counsellor occupies a 'favoured' position in the organization and the counsellor may feel some guilt from this type of perception. We have to remember that in some organizations, when redundancies are inevitable, personnel and counselling services are retained in order to provide what may seem to redundant employees like a veneer of care for their welfare.

The workplace counsellor on an ambiguous or temporary contract may have difficulty establishing effective relationships with key employees and with employee-clients because of the lack of a secure position, and this may have profound effects upon the counsellor and their work.

The second pressure can be the position of the workplace counsellor when it comes to reorganization, restructuring or job evaluation of teams, departments and individual employees. The counsellor is part of a system no matter how separately the counsellor attempts to position his or her service. The counsellor cannot ignore some of the dynamics of the system and is inevitably involved in many aspects of the 'politics' of an organization. Neither can the 'system' ignore the counsellor. The counsellor is part of a whole system. No permanent employees, especially those within the public sector, are exempt from being 're-organized'. An example of this is a public sector internal counselling service headed by an experienced EAP counsellor whose job was re-evaluated after 18 months of joining the organization and through the system it was down-graded, which involved a reduction of his salary. This had an impact on the individual and on the organization, who subsequently lost that counsellor. Another aspect is the evaluation of the post by non-counselling-related employees. In this example the system was objective about the whole process, but apparently there were no comparisons made with other such posts. The lesson from this is that a counsellor can easily be devalued or repositioned like any other employee – or over-valued and promoted like any other employee. Such uncertainty about a counsellor's future may not be a problem for the consellor in some organizations; however, in an insecure organization where job repositioning is frequent, then potentially the counsellor suffers the same pressure as all other employees.

Another feature of working as a counsellor in an organization is the presence of political values that may affect a counsellor on a personal as well as organizational level. In the public sector, a workplace counsellor may be a trade union member, and consequently required to act accordingly. This can result in workplace counsellors going on strike. Some large trade unions have a section for counsellors. This can be seen to be recognition that counsellors have rights and need protection of their terms and conditions like any other employee. But going on strike raises ethical dilemmas for many counsellors – do they put their own personal needs before the needs of a client or not? For counsellors who do not strike when employee-clients are on strike, what should they expect of their clients? Should they expect an employee-client to cross a picket line to attend a counselling session? These are dilemmas that have not been fully challenged or faced in the British counselling community, but may have to be as counselling in the workplace develops. It is a workplace issue that directly affects the counsellor as an employee.

CONCLUSION

A workplace counsellor, whether as an affiliate or as an in-house counsellor, has many relationships to 'hold in mind', to respect and negotiate in his or her everyday working life. Awareness of the importance of these relationships is crucial to the work that the counsellor does with employee-clients. Very often employees present with dysfunctional workplace relationships. A counsellor's understanding of his or her own personal workplace relationships can assist him or her to help an employee.

This chapter has shown how the workplace counsellor's role can be extended in a number of significant ways, enhancing not just the employing organization, but also the working life of the counsellor who wishes to move beyond the one-to-one counselling relationships that are his or her primary responsibility. Counselling in the workplace has come a long way, but there are concerns about its present position and the ways in which it might develop in future, and these are examined in the next chapter.

SIX

A critique of counselling in the workplace

We have by no means come to the end of our resources for combating the neuroses, and we may expect a substantial improvement in our therapeutic prospects before long. This reinforcement will come, I think, from three directions: (1) from internal progress (2) from increased authority, and (3) from the general effect of our work.

(Freud [1910a] 2001: 141)

Freud was addressing the Second Psycho-Analytical Congress in Nuremberg in 1910 when he proposed the three sources of development that would assist the progress of psychoanalysis. We can perhaps apply three similar sources to the future of workplace counselling: further research will assist in understanding what workplace counsellors do and what they achieve. Authority can be expanded by developing the profile of workplace counselling and creating professional counsellor-managers within this counselling setting. The more employees who access workplace counselling, the more its reputation will be advanced, but this also needs managing. Workplace counsellors need to be more active in promoting public understanding of what they are capable of achieving. Therefore, research, management training and publicity are required to develop and expand the use of workplace counselling in the UK.

As long as work continues to alienate people from themselves and each other, as long as work continues to be a convenient arena for the complex relationship struggles that we bring from our homes to our offices and factories, and as long as work reminds us of our past, there will be a place for counselling in the workplace. Counselling in the workplace will become as common as the first aid room, fire escapes and salary slips, unless counsellors decide otherwise, which they might, because counsellors are not well known as a group for their progressive views on society or for bringing about social change. Acutely focused on individuals, counsellors can fail to see what else is happening around them and some even fail to acknowledge that they may belong to a group of workers with common practices, values and ideas. As a counsellor coordinator in the NHS, I remember the loneliness and isolation that some counsellors said that they experienced working in that setting. Yet when it came to trying to arrange regular supportive meetings, only a small handful ever attended. For many counsellors, as long as no one interferes with their financial arrangements, which they like to keep secret, then they have no need to communicate with other counsellors, including their own colleagues. This may sound like a harsh judgement of many hard-working, highly trained and committed individuals, but it is relevant to discussing the future of workplace counselling. If counsellors enter organizations with previous experience of failing to work with others they will fail to be as effective in workplaces as they could be. Counselling in the workplace is different to counselling in other settings for a variety of reasons outlined in earlier chapters. But that is not all there is to say: we need to develop workplace counselling training courses that have merit and credibility to a wide audience and that are examination- and practice-based; to promote management training programmes for counsellors; to identify national standard systems of evaluation, to encourage research that has greater depth and is more accessible; and to foster broader professional bodies that have relevance to their membership and a greater sense of identity.

Other areas of growth for the future include:

- psychotherapy in the workplace and the development of long-term therapy that parallels employees' lives in organizations;
- counselling the organization – this is not a new idea, as psychoanalysts have been doing this in some quarters for decades;
- personal workplace therapy for counsellors in training – having personal therapy away from a workplace may not be appropriate for workplace training;
- employing more counsellors on the payroll rather than through subcontracting;
- developing more internal EAPs in the public sector.

The weaknesses and shortcomings of workplace counselling are the same as counselling problems in any other context; unclear and/or broken boundaries, lack of professional training, exploitation of clients, public ignorance, destructive competition and confusion between professional bodies.

COMPETITIVENESS

In the *Counselling and Psychotherapy Journal* (2002: 5) Feltham comments on the need for counsellors and psychotherapists to find 'greater convergence of approaches and practitioners'. This may help secure the future of counselling, yet on the letters page of the same journal there are examples of what happens to people after they have completed their counselling trainings. They are disappointed, alienated and financially 'out of pocket', because there are not the number of counselling jobs in the market place that they had perceived or had been led to expect. In some areas of the United Kingdom there is a surplus of counsellors, psychotherapists and practitioners. Such surplus creates competition, rivalry and envy among the counselling community. It can cause counsellors to lower their charges in private practice in order to attract clients and maintain basic income levels. As a result, many counsellors and psychotherapists feel that they have to devalue their work purely for economic reasons. There is ideological competition, which Feltham also refers to, and basic, crude, economic competition.

Ideological competition has been around since the beginning of the talking therapies, as Freud ([1925] 2001) experienced in many forms. Rivalry is around now. Rivalry and competition among therapists is not all bad, because it has the positive effect of promoting creativity and revision of dogmatic positions.

Competition also exists in the world of workplace counselling. It primarily manifests itself in economic rivalry between commercial EAPs. This is one of the problems that faces the EAPA UK – commercial sensitivity prevents open discussion about many issues that affect workplace counselling. For example, pricing of contracts between providers and purchasers, counsellors' rates of pay and problems with client-companies are not openly discussed in EAPA meetings. A clear reason for this is that most commercial EAPs are profit-led and do not wish to disclose any information that might benefit a rival. The consequence of this is that the EAPA UK sometimes is perceived as a trade organization that is muted by commercial sensitivity. It has produced standards and guidelines that are useful for prospective purchasers, and plans to develop accreditation standards for providers, but it has no statutory function. It can only refuse or rescind membership of the EAPA as a sanction, which does not necessarily have any long-term impact on a provider.

A secondary manifestation of competition, which may also have economic origins, is the debate about the difference between EAPs and workplace counselling services. There are important differences as many EAPs provide much more than counselling to employees. Many EAP workers are not counsellors and still provide excellent services to employees.

There are rivalries between workplace counselling services that are not necessarily based upon economic tensions. For example, the debate about internal versus external provision of counselling services is interesting. Are counselling services that are provided in-house by an employer more efficient than services that are delivered from outside an organization? This debate is similar to inter-tribal conflicts and family systems – should we let them in or keep them out? Whom can we trust? Who do we want to know about our business? Will they understand how we work? What will they do to us? These questions and other similar anxieties are brought into the debate about which is best – 'inside' or 'outside' counselling. McLeod (2001: 59) examines research on utilization of internal versus external services and finds that 'there is no clear trend in the direction of higher utilization in either external or internal programmes. This is a significant finding given the concern that is often expressed over the confidentiality of internal EAP/counselling provision, and the greater range of services typically offered by external providers.'

The inaugural meeting of a local authority counselling services discussion group in June 2002, comprising a variety of public sector professionals, was asked by a health and safety officer who was about to explore the possibilities of a counselling service for his local council, which was best – internal or external services? With one voice the meeting answered, 'Internal!' They favoured internal services for council employees, although some local authorities do have external commercial counselling services and EAPs. One of the reasons for this preference is the need to have some degree of control over the service and of management of the information that is provided by the service. There are also economic reasons. Internal counselling services are usually staffed by counsellors who are employees of the local authority. These local authority counsellors have a direct financial interest in maintaining the position of internal services, just as much as external EAP counsellors have commercial interests in promoting the benefits of external services.

CONFIDENTIALITY

There are problems with providing counselling in the workplace. The main boundary problem is between being confidential and independent while also being a fellow employee of the same company, being an affiliate who is paid indirectly by the employer or having other financial interests in the provision of counselling. Financial boundaries directly affect the confidentiality boundary. While many workplace counsellors try very hard to maintain ethical clarity about independence and confidentiality of their service, employees may perceive the service very differently. Often, it is the perception of the service by employee-clients that determines the success of the service. The position of the counsellor in an organization that can be so useful, unique and successful for employee-clients is also a source of the failure, under-usage and negative perception of a service. If a service is seen as being too close to management it will not be used by many employees. If a service is seen as being for the benefit of non-managerial employees only, it will not be used by managers. If the position of a service suggests that it is a management tool or if rumour in an organization suggests it is 'leaky' in the context of confidentiality, or simply 'no good', then it will not be used. Sometimes a service will be seen to be too close to other employees or serving other agendas. And sometimes a counselling service can be perceived as simply serving its own interests. Of course, these perceptions may be inaccurate or simply wrong, but they can 'damn' a service to failure. I know of one public sector example where an external service began to become irrelevant to employees after a period of years because it did not integrate with senior management, was staffed by ex-employees of the authority and offered too many different counselling models to employee-clients.

It is not easy entering an organization to become a workplace counsellor, as I have described previously. It can be compared to responding to a family who have asked for counselling help. The counsellor enters the family home, speaks to some of the family members and not to others while all the time being aware that many of the causes of the original problem are contained in the family home and within the family relationships. Does the counsellor become part of the family and potentially part of the problem? Can the counsellor remain separate enough from the family to help or not? These are the continuous challenges and difficulties that an internal or external counsellor has to face. Not every counsellor can do this and few training courses prepare counsellors for these complex tensions.

THE DOGMATIC COUNSELLOR

Other factors that affect the efficiency of a service are dogma and pedantry. Some counsellors dogmatically stick to theory and disregard the reality of the context in which they may apply some of the theory they have learnt. Many of the workplace counsellors that I have interviewed practise in the same way. They all had different training and were clear about their theoretical preferences, but in the workplace they apply the same methods and counselling techniques. The dominant concept is 'what will help this employee in six (four, eight, ten) sessions?' However, this is not a universal practice in workplace counselling, some counsellors believe that workplace counselling is simply an extension of private practice and all the theoretical rules and boundaries are identical. This leads some counsellors to ask 'how will this employee-client fit my practice?' Such a dogmatic approach will not be successful for many employee-clients, companies and EAPs.

A pedantic approach to a workplace counsellor is the other problem that stifles the success of a service. There are rigid systems that some EAPs impose upon counsellors that seem to demand excessive paperwork, reporting back and sometimes quite clearly to ask counsellors to behave unethically. Thankfully, the number of such reports from counsellors is low but it is a feature of workplace counselling provision and seems to be concentrated mainly, but not exclusively, in the insurance sector. Working with pedantic and overly controlling systems is difficult for many counsellors, however, and so if engaging in discussion with these companies about how to get the best from a workplace service for all involved does not improve things, the only other option for counsellors is not to work for that organization.

BEYOND THE COUNSELLING ROLE

An audit of a well-established commercial EAP provider is a useful source of information for understanding the reality of how counselling and EAPs within organizations are assessed. This audit was conducted by two individuals with EAP experience at the request of the purchaser, a public sector organization. The recommendations included administrative details which might assist an audit 'trail', such as: keeping copies of qualifications of telephone counsellors in their personnel files and copies of affiliate counsellors' qualifications in the EAP affiliate personnel file; visiting all counsellors' premises on a regular basis; and clarification from the purchaser about the period of time during which telephone calls should be answered, especially at weekends. While the recommendations appear to be primarily administrative, they also helped to develop the relationship between the purchaser and provider. In this audit, there was nothing overtly critical of the provision of the service by the EAP. Both parties in this contract were happy with the arrangement that was then in the fifth year of the contract. The audit, although pointing to some administrative details, simply reinforced the notion that it was a good idea for the purchaser to maintain the relationship with this EAP. But is this the extent of EAP auditing in the UK at present?

It is not possible 'just' to be a counsellor in a workplace counselling setting. Hill (2000) provides some excellent ideas about the extended benefits of a workplace counselling service from her experience as a counselling psychologist working in an NHS staff counselling service. She correctly points to the 'self limiting circularity in the discourse concerning workplace counselling' (2000: 13). As an antidote to organizational stress, workplace counselling has been aimed at helping individual employees recover once stress has been identified. It has not been seen as a proactive intervention for organizations, although the source that Hill quotes to suggest it should be is the Health and Safety Commission, rather than a counselling body such as the BACP, ACW or the EAPA. However, there are still many people in organizations who have no understanding of what counselling actually offers, and even fewer people who understand the potentially huge benefits that a workplace counselling service can bring about.

Hill uses three examples to show how workplace counselling can provide a 'micro-climate facilitating enhanced error management', 'enhance the sociotechnical design quality of the work system' and have an impact in 'enhancing organisational learning and development through creating an environment conducive to "double-loop" learning, and hence contribute to cultural change' (2000: 22). She acknowledges that there may be a variety of other factors that bring about cultural change, but the activities of the counsellors in the service she examined certainly contributed to the changes in the organization.

The activities of the counsellors went beyond the usual limitations of individual practice applied to an organizational setting, yet they maintained the essential elements of good counselling practice such as confidentiality, respect and patient listening. The counsellors became involved in small group work, team sessions and helping middle managers develop a management forum. This was in addition to the work with individual employees that also helped bring about important changes for the organization. This leads Hill to add to her conclusions that

> Some of the processes and functions of counselling in a workplace setting may be re-framed in terms of models of organisational change, organisational design, organisational learning, performance management or human resource management. Such re-framing might serve both to de-mystify the activity of counselling and also render the roles of Counsellors and Counselling Psychologists more amenable to integration within organisational and management theory and practice.
>
> (Hill 2000: 23)

Hill identifies the possible development and future of workplace counselling as well as the one factor that may prevent such growth – the counsellors themselves. Some workplace counsellors, and workplace counselling services, do not want additional functions or for anyone else in the organization to understand what they do. However, other workplace counsellors are actively carrying out a multitude of roles and functions every day in organizations that are glad to use such multifunctional employees. Carroll (1996: 50) refers to research that identified 19 separate functions described by 12 different in-house workplace counsellors. He adds that he believes a counselling role is incompatible with a managerial role, and cannot 'belong together in the same person' (1996: 51).

I would add another four functions and roles to those described by Carroll; the workplace counsellor has a role as an employee (or affiliate/subcontractor or self-employed counsellor attached to the organization); colleague to other employees; supervisee; and, for some counsellors, patient or client if they are in personal therapy as part of their role. This applies in some prison services – counsellors are expected to be in personal therapy while they do their job and they receive an allowance towards the cost of personal therapy.

Part of the attraction for some counsellors working in organizations is the variety of tasks. Belbin (1993) developed the concept of different roles in a work group, and perhaps there are different 'counselling types' that find different settings? The variety and changes within organizational life may suit a particular type of counsellor.

An example of a workplace counselling service similar to the service Hill (2000) describes is a large British public sector organization, where the diary of the experienced EAP manager, a psychodynamic counsellor, shows the different demands, roles and functions he enjoys in his work – although some weeks are difficult because of having to focus on too great a variety of tasks. However, fortnightly supervision helps maintain a healthy balance between clinical and non-clinical work.

It is worth asking what happens when counsellors take up non-counselling roles in organizations? A counsellor's effective life in an organization may be limited for a number of reasons: lack of career opportunities; 'burn-out'; personal development of the counsellor; organizational pressures; and the wrong home–work balance. Fatigue and burn-out are probably the most common causes of counsellors changing roles, especially when these factors coincide with a career opportunity. For example, a senior counsellor had a managerial position in an NHS staff counselling scheme. Her marketing and policy work was noticeable to other senior managers and she was encouraged to apply for an organizational development post. This post took her away from the front-line management of the counselling service and developed her managerial and strategic skills and abilities, which were put to good use by the institution. One of her reasons for applying for the post was because she had been managing counsellors and working with individuals for a long period of time and needed a change and a fresh challenge. She was fortunate, as not every workplace counsellor has such opportunities or encouragement. However, a workplace counsellor may have access to more opportunities than a private practice counsellor when looking for a career change. The disadvantage may be that workplace counsellors sometimes know too much about employees, managers and the organization to be promoted to a more senior position.

JUDGING BY RESULTS

Arthur (2000) suggests that EAPs do not deliver everything that they promise in terms of increased production, reduced absenteeism and further cost savings to the companies that they sell their services to. In particular, when EAPs are asked to deliver stress training programmes, seminars or relaxation sessions all that happens is reinforcement of the concept that stress is an individual employee problem and not an organizational issue. Arthur states that the little research that has been done into stress management delivery by EAPs provides two conclusions: first, that while counsellors and employees report relief from symptoms, this does not necessarily have any impact upon the organization itself; second, sometimes there is an increase in stress-related symptoms! One experienced workplace counsellor suggested that if the counsellor is successful, employees will leave an unhealthy organization, and that the measure of counselling success may be the number of clients who quit their jobs. There is some truth in this idea. Equally, counsellors may collude with unhealthy organizations and maintain employees in unsuitable jobs, professions and working lives because they are paid to do so – it may be part of an unspoken deal between an organization and the counsellor it employs. So counsellors can become part of the alienation process – temporarily taking care of the soul that the employee-client sells to the organization, and simultaneously selling out themselves to their employer.

SUPPLY AND DEMAND?

Another question that needs to be raised about workplace counselling is the current demand for counsellors in companies and institutions compared to the number of counsellors available. One EAP clinical director predicted that the counselling market in the United Kingdom would be flooded with counsellors and that the market would begin to sort out those who would remain in the industry and those who be forced to find other employment. He cited the NHS as an example of a sector where counsellors are gradually being replaced by nurse specialists, psychology graduates and GPs doing their own counselling rather than paying £20,000 to £30,000 for a counsellor in their practice. He wondered where all the newly qualified counsellors would go – where will they work? Who will employ them? He speculated that perhaps there will be more small private businesses who will begin to use counsellors on a casual basis for their employees, and he hoped that the growth of public sector internal services would be a useful setting for counsellors looking for work. In North America, one of the largest EAPs made redundancies among their counsellors and the unions withdrew up to 400 members from the EAPA – although this may have involved other issues. Other individuals within the UK counselling world also predict that counselling is reaching a peak and that the market is saturated.

What does this mean for workplace counselling? It means that workplace counselling has to adapt and evolve in ways that will assist in the development of these important services. Counsellors need to be trained as managers if they are in managerial positions, and they need to provide depth and further understanding to organizations about what happens in the workplace.

MANAGEMENT TRAINING FOR COUNSELLORS

Experienced and highly trained counsellors do not necessarily make 'good enough' managers. The core skills of workplace counselling are not always transferable into another function such as management. This is a phenomenon that Egan often talks about and seems to be a universal problem. Usually 'management' is not regarded as a separate profession, vocation or function. People are promoted to managerial positions in many organizations without any management training or aptitude and then they are expected to be managers and manage other employees. Egan uses a medical comparison that emphasizes this point: lying on a trolley awaiting surgery, Egan was approached by the man who said he was going to be the surgeon operating on him that day. Egan asked him how long he had been a surgeon and the man replied 'Oh, not long; I was so good as the head of the maintenance department that I was promoted to being a surgeon'. The point is not so ironic when applied to real management careers in many organizations. Many managers are in positions of authority by default not by merit, management training or experience.

Egan makes another point about poor management often being the cause of many workplace problems for managers and non-managers alike. He asks: if an employee has a medical problem would the employee's manager be expected to provide assistance medically? There might perhaps be a referral to occupational health, the company doctor or nurse, but nothing more than that. If the same employee has a psychological difficulty, for example depression, why is the manager expected to do something about this? Exploration of work factors and relationships that are contributing to an employee's depression may have to be taken up by the manager, but there is perhaps an over-expectation of what managers can do to help employees with mental health problems.

What produces this expectation and what does it mean? Why is so much expected from so many who have such little training and skills? It is partly because managers consciously and unconsciously take on important positions in organizations as scapegoats or as authority figures, loaded with different fantasies, and become the focus for a huge variety of individual and organizational projections, fears and defences. Taking on a mental health role as a manager is similar to taking on the role as a counsellor. The difference is that a counsellor has a different experience of authority and power – no less authority, but a different use of power. The counsellor helps the client find their own power, whereas the manager tends to impose their power – one gives, the other takes control. The counsellor usually helps the client to access their authority for their own benefit, whereas the manager uses their authority for the benefit of the organization. The counsellor is perhaps more consciously aware of being set up as a focus for projection, as this will have been learnt in the counsellor's training. This is a subject worthy of cross-fertilization in management and counselling training, and it is addressed in some training programmes such as the organizational courses offered by the Tavistock Consultancy Services (TCS). The findings of the Tavistock courses and approach should be integrated into current counselling training courses. Perhaps new workplace training courses can incorporate these valuable and relevant concepts. The TCS provide a variety of courses that cover the subjects of management and leadership, senior executive coaching and managing change in organizations. All of these ideas can be helpful and directly relevant to the function of workplace counselling.

A common factor in the positions of counsellor and manager in an organization is that they are set apart from other employees, and as such can become screens onto which other employees can project their fantasies, sometimes counsellors and managers also set themselves up to take on these roles. Being set apart from other employees or clients may be important in order to establish a professional working relationship, although the 'distance' between a client and counsellor is different from that between a manager and a subordinate. But the positions of counsellor and manager may have some common features that can be explored further in a management course for counsellors.

A common feature of many workplace counselling services is the provision of 'counselling skills' courses delivered by counsellors to non-counsellors and sometimes specifically designed for managers. It is usually considered part of the service that counsellors can provide and is often well received. But this skill cross-over is seldom reciprocated. It would be interesting to know how often counsellors are offered management skills training, or one-to-one managerial mentoring or coaching for their managerial role. One clinical director in a large EAP tells how valuable management training was to him and helped him to see counselling as part of a bigger world so that he could deliver a counselling service within a commercial setting and within the constraints of commercial reality.

There have been many fashions and 'fads' in research into management training, producing multiple contradictory messages about management as Guest (1996: 274) points out. But the management system that Egan produces in 'adding value' (1993) is a useful framework. Egan asserts that managers 'are usually not neutral. They add either net value or cost' (1993: 10).

COUNSELLING THE ORGANIZATION

Organizational consultants providing insight, guidance and a reflective structure for senior employees in organizations have been around for a long time. Carroll describes counselling the organization as a product of organizational consultancy that involves a broader exploration of the whole of the organization within its context – for example, how does a local authority relate to other organizations and groups within its geographical boundary? This is a similar approach to helping an individual look at various familial relationships in his or her life, or helping a manager explore team dynamics. Tehrani (2001 paper) has used similar principles to explore the personality of a large public sector organization. She applied a mental health diagnosis of schizophrenia to a council that struggled to meet the complex, ambiguous and contradictory demands of its existence and of a service that was required by many different and competing masters. The struggle resulted in a schizophrenic organization that became so disturbed it was unable to function at any useful level. Her example of a local authority differed from private sector and voluntary organizations because the latter's remits are more straightforward and clear – they deliver products and services as required and are either profit or non-profit in their function. A counsellor working with the organization as their client may help with such complex demands.

Carroll and Walton outline this role:

> If as workplace counsellors we are to become relevant, inte-grated and part of an organisation, we do not need to contort ourselves into becoming Organisational Development experts, HR or Personnel Directors, advisers to managers, etc. All we need to do is what we do best as counsellors and apply it to the organisation as well as the individual client.
>
> (Carroll and Walton 1997: 106)

Carroll (2002, private communication) identifies the skills that counsellors, psychologists and psychotherapists have and groups them together in a list:

- we look to process;
- we make connections (e.g. past, present, future);

- we stay with pain;
- we work with emotions and feelings;
- we set up healthy relationships (boundaries, no abuse etc);
- we allow the other person to set the agenda;
- we facilitate lasting change.

When a counsellor or therapist enters an organization and uses these processes and techniques then Carroll refers to them as 'counselling consultants'. He insists that all of the above skills have to be used, and if they are not then the process is something different – mentoring, coaching or using counselling skills. He counsels individuals, teams and organizations in the same way.

Carroll provides an example of how he works. With a colleague, he was working with a team of 50 people. They met with all the team members individually for 45 minutes each to listen to their stories, and a report was written that summarized the current position of the team. Carroll and his colleague had established healthy relationships with the team, made some important connections with them, started to work with some of the pain and different emotions in the team and followed the team's agenda. The next stage was to look at further interventions and discussion of changes possible within the team. Although this activity was called 'team development' by the organization, he refers to it as a counselling intervention by two organizational counsellors.

Stress audits are different. They have a definite aim: to identify or confirm 'stress' in a team or organization. One of the problems with stress audits is the lack of follow-up that seems to occur after a report is submitted where it confirms stress is present in a team. In one organization, reports were filed with senior managers of teams and departments and then the senior manager was left to implement the changes identified without any further assistance, guidance or organizational counselling.

Palmer describes the 'Tavistock paradigm' (2002: 158) which includes the work of practitioners from the Tavistock Institute and Clinic with a variety of organizations over many years. The basic elements of the work carried out by consultants attached to the Tavistock can also be applied to counsellors working psychodynamically with organizations. Palmer outlines the basic elements: working with groups; being a container for client anxieties; working with transference and counter-transference; working through boundaries; working interpretatively; and using experiential learning techniques and events.

An extension of the Tavistock-style consultancy is 'conflict resolution' as developed particularly by Linda Hambleton and the Tavistock Consultancy Service. Although not counselling, many counselling skills are used in this active mediation, conciliation and facilitation process that has been introduced into many British organizations since 1996. Knowledge of psychoanalytic, sociotechnical and systems theory helps in delivering this service to employees. The 'mediator' helps employees resolve a workplace conflict using a variety of techniques and is predominantly interested in the process of the resolution rather than as content. The mediator takes a 'neutral' position between the two employees, who need to volunteer to take part in the process. The mediator gives a short introduction to the two employees who are sat at a table facing each other, with the mediator sat in the middle and not facing either of them but clearly turning to speak to each one. This is a highly stylized form of negotiation that is not intended to be a counselling relationship, but is an extension of counselling skills.

Hopkins urges workplace counsellors to assist organizations at a different level but 'it is not our role to take on the mantle of the classic management consultant. Our role should be to help companies with the source of stress rather than just the symptoms' (1998: 3).

CONCLUSION

Providing care and help for employees has come a long way from Florence Boot giving cups of coffee and hot chocolate to women arriving at work in the morning. Todays' EAPs and counselling services are sophisticated, well organized and profitable for all involved. Offering a counselling service to employees is a brave and now necessary undertaking for employers. It is brave because it is recognition that work can cause huge difficulties for individuals and that the employer has some responsibility for some of these problems. Perhaps contemporary employers are discreetly acknowledging Marx's concept of alienation and while being the cause of this, are simultaneously offering opportunities for addressing it through counselling. The life of many an employee has been rescued by counsellors in workplaces, and many organizations have been able to retain important employees because of counselling interventions. Equally, many employees have been able to make important decisions for themselves and left abusive employers thanks to the help of workplace counsellors.

There are many successful counselling services in workplaces that continue to develop ways of helping employees. I believe it is crucial for counsellors to continually look creatively at their functions in the workplaces and to look to expand services to employees while maintaining their professional integrity. Counsellors do not need to become 'jack of all trades' in the workplace, but their insight and reflection can help organizations to develop better systems, better management and better places to work if feedback is expressed in the right way to the right people. This entails counsellors developing different broader organizational perspectives. There are many different ways of doing this – for example, using the methods of the Tavistock Consultancy Service, the National Local Authority Group for the Development of Counselling and through the development of the ACW and EAPA UK.

As I write the pioneers of workplace counselling in Britain and the United States are still active and continue to add to the knowledge and depth of applying counselling to this unique setting. This is both an indication of the relatively young age of counselling in the workplace and of the way it is still opening up new avenues. It is an exciting field to work in, one which brings counsellors into contact with the realities of the business and commercial world and with the major institutions that underpin the welfare of millions of people. In many ways the consulting room and shop floor are next to each other. Both have much to gain and learn from each other. Gone are the days of the small consulting room with the door firmly shut against the external world, and the deliberate concentration on the inner world of the client. In workplace counselling, therapy has come out of the consulting room to face up to the exigencies of people's working lives and the strengths and weaknesses of commercial organizations. What we in this setting hope for is that counsellors working in other settings, particularly with individuals in their independent practices, will learn from the pioneering work of this relatively young part of the profession; and that those who are responsible for the welfare of employees (as well as for their own) can learn from the values that have informed therapists and helped them to forge new ways of understanding how people and organizations work.

Appendix I

NORTH STAFFORDSHIRE COMBINED HEALTHCARE NHS TRUST

STAFF COUNSELLING SERVICE

CLIENT ASSESSMENT

CLIENT REGISTRATION NUMBER _____

Personal Details

Marital	Single		Married		Separated		Divorced	
Status	Widow		Widower		Partner		Not available	
Client Ethic Origin	White		Black		Asian		Other	
Age			Sex	Male			Female	

Work Information

Occupation By Category

Occupation by category	1 Community Nursing (including CPN, Health Visitor etc)		6 Senior Manager		11 Medical (Doctors)	
	2 Hospital Nurse		7 Admin & Clerical		12 Student/Cadet Nurse	
	3 Health Care Support Worker		8 Support Services (porters, domestics, catering, hairdressing etc)		13 Other - please specify	
	4 Nurse Manager (including Ward Manager, Clinical Nurse Specialist, House Manager)		9 Qualified PAMS (Professions Allied to Medicine (OT's, Physio, Speech Therapist etc)			
	5 Department Managers (non-clinical)		10 Unqualified PAMS (OT/Physio assistants etc)			

Location - North Staffs Combined Healthcare Only

Directorate (please circle)	MH	LD	PC	EC	Other (please state):
Place of work	**Department**			**Hospital/Community** (please circle)	

Location - Other than NSCH Employees

Employer - Please circle			
North Staffs Health Authority	**Staffs Moorlands PCG**	**South Stoke PCT**	**Staffs Moorlands District Council**
Occupation	**Place of Work**		**Department**

Special conditions (ie not to be contacted at work, not to arrive with another client etc)

Special Instructions	

Referral to Staff Counselling Service Information

How did they hear about us?	1 Personal Recommendation		2 Human Resources		3 Occupational Health	
	4 Line Manager		5 Senior Manager		6 Trade Union	
	7 Presentation/Induction		8 Brochure		9 Newsline	
	10 Workshop		11 Previous Experience		12 Other	

Initial Dates/Appointments/Contracting Information

Date of initial contact			
Date of assessment		Time	
Counsellor			
Location			
No of initial sessions agreed		Contract Limit	CHC 8	Others	6
No of further sessions (Agreed at Case Management Mtgs)	Date/Number	Date/Number	Date/Number	Date/Number

Presenting Problems	
Personal	Work

Current Life Situation	Underlying Issues Note any relevant underlying issues or distressing life events since childhood.
1 Family/Relationships	
2 Social Life	
3 Physical Health/Current Medication	
	*CLIENT AT RISK PROTOCOL ***Inform manager immediately**
4 GP Name/Address	▪ Has client expressed suicidal thoughts/intentions to self harm? ▪ Do you have concerns about safety of others connected to this client?
5 GP Tel No	▪ Do you feel the client needs access to medical/psychiatric services eg drugs, alcohol, bereavement?

Summary of issues and focus of Counselling

PRESENTING PROBLEM - WORK PROBLEMS (Please tick appropriate box)

1. Work-related stress i.e. lack of support/control, high demands vs perceived ability to cope		2. GP diagnosed depression/ anxiety (Please circle)	Y N	3. Work Relationship Problems		4. Harassment	
Investigation - Yes/No (Please tick appropriate box below)							
5. Grievance		6. Disciplinary			7. Complaint		
8. Other Work Problems (Please be specific)							

PRESENTING PROBLEM - PERSONAL PROBLEMS
(Please tick appropriate box)

7. Substance Misuse		8. Loss/ Bereavement		9. OCD (eg anorexia)		10. Health problems	
11. Personal Relationship		12. Domestic Violence		13. Family Problems			

14. Other personal problems (please be specific)

Appointment dates/DNA records

(This session must be completed after each session whether the client attends or not).

Details of Counselling	Session	Date	Attended	Cancelled	DNA
Appointments	1				
	2				
	3				
Review*	4				
	5				
	6				
End	7				
Follow Up	8				

* Review at 3/4 session.   End at 7th.   Follow up at 8th.

No further appointments to agreed Case Management decision.

Discharge Information

For completion by Counsellor

Termination Date		Total number of sessions	
Referred to other agency (Please specify agency)		Date of referral to other agency	

Termination Comments

Evaluation - Counsellor Confirmation

Evaluation Given At Last Session (Please circle Y or N and add date)	If no, please circle where evaluation was sent and add date
Yes/No	Home/Work

Counsellors please confirm:

Description	Date & Initials
Notes and file removed from cabinet	
Termination details completed	
Termination entered into register	
Evaluation process completed	
Notes placed into termination file	

Administrator please confirm

Termination completed on database	
Notes filed in termination drawer	
Session notes shredded (to be agreed with Service Manager prior to shredding	

Appendix II

NORTH STAFFORDSHIRE COMBINED HEALTHCARE NHS TRUST

STAFF COUNSELLING SERVICE

SERVICE EVALUATION FORM

Counsellor Ref No	

Evaluation Questionnaire

We would greatly appreciate your help in evaluating the counselling service by filling in this questionnaire. All replies are confidential and results will be presented only as general statements. Please tick or circle the appropriate answer.

First Impressions

1 **Did you find it easy to make contact with the service by telephone?**   Yes/No

If the answer is No please tick the most appropriate answer:-

Tried 2/3 times	Took 3 times or more	Left message	Other (Please state)

2 **Did the Counselling Service Administrator help put you at ease?**   Yes/No

Comments: _____

3 **Was the function of the service explained to you by the administrator and were you offered a brochure/ information?**   Yes/No

Comments: _____

Questions about the service in general

Please tick as appropriate

	Poor	Fair	Good	Very Good	Excellent
4 How would you rate the quality of the service you received?					

Would you recommend the service to others	Yes		No	

Questions about the counsellor

5 **Again please answer the following questions by ticking the most appropriate box.**

	Very Untrue	Untrue	Not Sure	True	Very True
I felt I could trust my counsellor to be open and honest with me					
I did not have much faith in my counsellor					
My counsellor understood my problem(s)					
My counsellor helped me to understand my issues more clearly					
I thought my counsellor and I established a good working relationship					
I thought my counsellor was too challenging					
My counsellor seemed uncomfortable when I talked about certain things					
My counsellor was friendly and at ease					
My counsellor was concerned for me					
My counsellor helped me handle issues better as a result of being with her/him					
I am very pleased to have had the opportunity to be with this counsellor					

Questions on how counselling has had an influence on your life:

6a   **How has counselling helped improve your working life? Please specify:**

_____

_____

6b   **How has counselling helped improve your personal life? Please specify:**

_____

_____

7   **Was the problem that brought you to counselling** (please tick one box only):-

A work issue [   ]   A personal issue [   ]   Both [   ]

8   **Would you have liked:-**

More sessions [   ]   Fewer sessions [   ]   Just right [   ]

9   **As a result of your problem(s) were you off work at any time? If <u>yes</u> did using the Staff Counselling Service contribute to your ability to return to work?**

Comments: _____

_____

10   **If you had <u>no</u> time off work, do you feel that you were able to continue working during your difficulties because of the support that you received from the Staff Counselling Services?**

Comments: _____

_____

Future Services

We are investigating the possibility of a Telephone Counselling Helpline which will be available for staff to call out of office hours eg 3 hours each evening 5 days per week Monday–Friday and 3 hours each morning Saturday and Sunday. Please state whether you think this is a service that you would use or recommend to others:

Comments: _____

Please let us know of any further comments you would like to make, or any changes you would like to see in the Staff Counselling Service.

_____

_____

_____

_____

_____

Thank you for your help. Please return the questionnaire in the envelope provided.

References

ACA (American Counseling Association) (1995) *Code of Ethics and Practice*. Baltimore: ACA.

ACA (American Counseling Association) (2002) Definition of professional counseling: www.counseling.org/join aca/definition.htm (accessed 27 January 2002).

Addenbrooke's NHS Trust (2002) Work–life balance home page: www. addenbrookes.org.uk/hr/worklife1.html (accessed 25 May 2002).

Adler, A. (1932) *What Life Should Mean To You*. London: Unwin Books.

Amaral, T.M. (1999) Benchmarks and performance measures for employee assistance programmes, in J. Oher (ed.) *The Employee Assistance Handbook*. New York: John Wiley and Sons.

Arthur, A. (2000) Employee assistance programmes: the emperors new clothes and stress management, *British Journal of Guidance and Counselling*, 28(4).

Arthur, A. (2001) Employee assistance programs. Do they work? *EAP Association Exchange*, July/August, 31(4).

Axelrod, S.D. (1999) *Work and the Evolving Self*. London: The Analytic Press.

BACP (British Association for Counselling and Psychotherapy) (2002) *Ethical Framework for Good Practice in Counselling and Psychotherapy*. Rugby: BACP.

Belbin, M. (1993) Team Roles at Work. Oxford: Butterworth–Heinemann.

Bond, T. (2000) *Standards and Ethics For Counselling In Action*. London: Sage.

Briner, R. (2000) Do EAPs work? *Counselling At Work*, 37.

Butler, C. (1999) Organizational Counselling: the profession's shadow side, *Counselling*, 10(3).

Cagney, T. (1999) Models of service delivery, in J. Oher (ed.) *The Employee Assistance Handbook*. New York: John Wiley and Sons.

Carroll, M. (1996) *Workplace Counselling*. London: Sage.

Carroll, M. (1998) Integrated, isolated or irrelevant? in L. Macwhinnie (ed.) *Counselling At Work*. Rugby: BACP.

Carroll, M. and Walton, M. (1997) *The Handbook of Counselling in Organizations*. London: Sage.

CEPEC (Centre for Professional Employment Counselling) (1985) *Counselling News for Managers*. CEPEC.

CMCA (CEPEC Managers Counselling Association) (1987) *Information Leaflet*. CMCA.

Cooper, J. and Alfille, H. (1998) *Assessment In Psychotherapy*. London: Karnac Books.

Cooper, C.L. and Highley-Marchington, J.C. (1998) *An Assessment of Employee Assistance and Workplace Counselling Programmes in British Organisations*. Manchester: HSE and UMIST.

CORE System Group (1998) *CORE System (Information Management) Handbook*. Leeds: CORE System Group. (http://www.coreims.co.uk).

Court of Appeal (2002) http://porch.ccta.gov.uk/courtser/judgements.nsf/5cbcc578co1a/Sutherland v Hatton.ht (accessed 12 February 2002).

Czander, W. (1993) *The Psychodynamics of Work and Organisations. Theory and Application*. New York: Guildford Press.

Darick, A.A. (1999) Clinical practices and procedures, in J. Oher (ed.) *The Employee Assistance Handbook*. New York: John Wiley and Sons.

Davidson, B.N. and Herlihy, P.A. (1999) The EAP and work–family connection, in J. Oher (ed.) *The Employee Assistance Handbook*. New York: John Wiley and Sons.

EAPA UK (Employee Assistance Professionals Association, UK) (1998) *UK Guidelines for Audit and Evaluation for Employee Assistance Programmes*. Rugby: EAPA.

EAPA UK (Employee Assistance Professionals Association, UK) (2000) *UK Standards of Practice and Professional Guidelines for Employee Assistance Programmes*. Rugby: EAPA.

EAPA UK (Employee Assistance Professionals Association, UK) (2001) Meeting, August (unpublished paper). Rugby: EAPA.

EAPA UK (Employee Assistance Professionals Association, UK) (2002) Internal document. Rugby: EAPA.

Egan, G. (1993) *Adding Value*. San Francisco: Josey-Bass Publishers.

Egan, G. (2001) Paper presented at the A Day in the Life of a Public Sector Employee Conference, Northampton, December.

Egan, G. (2002) *The Skilled Helper*, 7th edn. Pacific Grove: Wadsworth Group.

Evans, C., Connell, J., Barkham, M. *et al.* (2002) Towards a standardised brief outcome measure: psychometric properties and utility of the CORE-OM, *British Journal of Psychiatry*, 180: 51–60.

Feltham, C. (1997) *The Gains of Listening*. Buckingham: Open University Press.

Feltham, C. (2002) The benefits of therapy, *Counselling and Psychotherapy Journal*, 13(9).

Freud, S. ([1910] 2001a) *The Future Prospects of Psycho-analytic Therapy*, Standard edition, Vol. 11. London: Vintage.

Freud, S. ([1910] 2001b) *Leonardo Da Vinci and a Memory of his Childhood*, Standard edition, Vol. 11. London: Vintage.

Freud, S. ([1913] 2001) *On Beginning the Treatment*, Standard edition, Vol. 12. London: Vintage.

Freud, S. ([1919] 2001) *Lines of Advance in Psychoanalytic Therapy*, Standard edition, Vol. 17. London: Vintage.

Freud, S. ([1921] 2001) *Group Psychology and the Analysis of the Ego*, Standard edition, Vol. 18. London: Vintage.

Freud, S. ([1925] 2001) *An Autobiographical Study*, Standard edition, Vol. 20. London: Vintage.

Freud, S. ([1927] 2001) *The Future of an Illusion*, Standard edition, Vol. 21. London: Vintage.

Freud, S. ([1930] 2001) *Civilisation and its Discontents*, Standard edition, Vol. 21. London: Vintage.

Freud, S. ([1937] 2001) *Analysis Terminable and Interminable*, Standard edition, Vol. 23. London: Vintage.

Freud, S. ([1938] 2001) *An Outline of Psychoanalysis*, Standard edition, Vol. 23. London : Vintage.

Fromm, E. (1970) *The Crisis of Psychoanalysis*. Harmondsworth: Penguin.

Furnham, A. (1999) *The Psychology of Behaviour at Work*. Hove: Psychology Press.

Gabriel, L. (2002) Working in a multi-task job, *Counselling and Psychotherapy Journal*, 13(4): 5.

Gabriel, Y. (ed.) (1999) *Organizations in Depth*. London: Sage.

Galliano, S. (2002) Debriefing reconsidered, *Counselling and Psychotherapy Journal*, 13(2): 20–1.

Gay, P. (1994) *Freud. A Life For Our Time*. London: Papermac.

Goss, S. and Rose, S. (2002) Evidence based practice: a guide for counsellors and psychotherapists, *Counselling and Psychotherapy Research*, 2(2).

Gray, A. (1994) *An Introduction to the Therapeutic Frame*. London: Routledge.

Greenson. R. (1967) *The Technique and Practice of Psychoanalysis*. London: Hogarth Press.

Guest, D. (1996) Leadership and management, in P. Warr (ed.) *Psychology At Work*. London: Penguin.

Haverkamp, B. and Paposki, D. (2000) Interdisciplinary collaboration: ethical issues and recommendations, *Canadian Journal of Counselling*, 34(2): 85–6.

Hill, C. (2000) Does workplace counselling have an organisational function? *Counselling Psychology Review*, 15(4): 13.

Hirschorn, L. (1999) Leaders and followers, in Y. Gabriel (ed.) *Organizations In Depth*. London: Sage.

Hirschorn, L. (2000) *The Workplace Within*. Massachusetts: MIT Press.

Hood, V. (1995) Work-related counselling – a psychodynamic approach, *Psychodynamic Counselling*, 1(2): 248.

Hopkins, V. (1998) Is counselling for the organization or employee? in L. Macwhinnie (ed.) *Counselling At Work*. Rugby: BACP.

Jacobs, M. (1991) *Psychodynamic Counselling In Action*. London: Sage.

Jacobs, M. (2000) The use of contracts in the psychodynamic/psychoanalytic approach, in C. Sills (ed.) *Contracts In Counselling*. London: Sage.

Jenkins, P. (2002) Whatever you say is confidential, but . . ., *Counselling and Psychotherapy Journal*, 13(2): 10.

Jones, E. (1962) *The Life and Works of Sigmund Freud*. Harmondsworth: Penguin.

Kennedy, E. and Charles, S. (1990) *On Becoming A Counsellor*. Dublin: Gill and Macmillan.

Kets de Vries, M. (1987) *The Neurotic Organisation*. San Francisco: Jossey-Bass.

Kierkegaard, S. (1959) *Either/Or*. New York: Anchor Books.

Lago, C. and Kitchin, D. (1998) *The Management of Counselling Agencies*. London: Sage.

Langs, R. (1998) *Ground Rules In Psychotherapy and Counselling*. London: Karnac Books.

Laplanche, J. and Pontalis, J-B. (1988) *The Language of Psychoanalysis*. London: Karnac Books.

Leiper, R. (2000) *The Unconscious At Work*. Philadelphia: Brunner-Routledge.

McInnes, B. (2002) Editorial, *Counselling At Work*, 37(1).

McLellan, D. (1972) *Karl Marx. Early Texts*. Oxford: Blackwell.

McLeod, J. (1998) *An Introduction to Counselling*. Buckingham: Open University Press.

McLeod, J. (2001) *Counselling in the Workplace: The Facts*. Rugby: BACP.

Malan, D. (2001) *Individual Psychotherapy and the Science of Psychodynamics*. London: Arnold.

Mander, G. (2000) *A Psychodynamic Approach to Brief Therapy*. London: Sage.

Marx, K. (1844) Estranged labour, *Karl Marx and Frederick Engels Collected Works*, Vol. 3. London. Lawrence and Wishart.

Mellor-Clark, J. (2001a) Advances in measuring the effectiveness of workplace counselling, unpublished paper presented at the ACW autumn conference, London, 23 November.

Mellor-Clark, J. (2001b) How can quality be enhanced in counselling services? in B. Bower, J. Foster and J. Mellor-Clark (eds) *Quality in Counselling in Primary Care: A Guide for Effective Commissioning and Clinical Governance*. Manchester: NPCRDC.

Mellor-Clark, J. (2002) A CORE profile for counselling in primary care. *Psychiatry*, 1: 4, 39–43.

Mellor-Clark, J., Barkham, M., Connell, J. and Evans, C. (1999) Practice-based evidence and the need for a standardised evaluation system: informing the design of the CORE System, *European Journal of Psychotherapy, Counselling and Health*, 2: 357–74.

Mellor-Clark, J. and Barkham, M. (2000) Accountability and quality assurance, in C. Feltham and I. Horton (eds) *The Handbook of Counselling*. London: Sage.

Molnos, A. (1995) *A Question Of Time*. London: Karnac Books.

Munroe, R. (1956) *Psychoanalytic Thought*. New York: Dryden Press.

Munt, S. (2000) The EAP trap. *Counselling*, 11(7): 419.

North Staffordshire Combined NHS Healthcare Trust (2002) Annual report, Staff Counselling Service, internal document.

O'Carroll, L. (2002) Do we make a difference? *Counselling and Psychotherapy Journal*, July, 13(6): 11.

Oher, J. (ed.) (1999) *The Employee Assistance Handbook*. New York: John Wiley and Sons.

Oher, J., Conti, D. and Jongsman, A. (1998) *The Employee Assistance Treatment Planner*. New York: John Wiley and Sons.

Palmer, B. (2002) The Tavistock paradigm: inside, outside and beyond, in R.D. Hinshelwood and M. Chiesa (eds) *Organisations, Anxieties and Defences*. London: Whurr Publishers.

Paproski, D. and Haverkamp, B. (2000) Interdisciplinary collaboration: ethical issues and recommendations, *Canadian Journal of Counselling*, 34(2).

Parlett, M. and Page, F. (1990) Transactional analysis, in W. Dryden (ed.) *Individual Therapy: A Handbook*. Buckingham: Open University Press.

Reddy, M. (1998) *The Manager's Guide to Counselling at Work*. London: British Psychological Society and Methuen.

Robinson, S. (2002) What gets measured gets delivered, *Psychoanalytic Psycho Therapy*, 16(1): 37–57.

Rogers, C. (1951) *Client-centered Therapy*. London: Constable.

Rogers, C. (1980) *On Becoming a Person*. London: Constable.

Rose, S. and Goss, S. (2002) Evidence based practice: a guide for counsellors and psychotherapists, *Counselling and Psychotherapy Research*, 2(2).

Scott, M. and Stradling, S. (1998) *Counselling for Post-Traumatic Stress Disorder*. London: Sage.

Sonnenstuhl, W. (1986) *Inside An Emotional Health Program*. New York: ILR Press.

Sonnenstuhl, W. and Trice, H.M. (1995) *Strategies For Employee Assistance Programs: The Crucial Balance*. New York: ILR Press.

Steele, D.P. (1989) A history of job based alcoholism programs: 1955–1972, *Journal of Drug Issues*, 19(4): 511–32.

Steele, D.P. and Trice, H. (1995) A history of job based alcoholism programs: 1972–1980, *Journal of Drug Issues*, 398.

Sutherland v. Hatton (2002) Court of Appeal, Neutral Citation Number
    EWCA   Civ   76:   http://porch.ccta.gov.uk/courtser/judgements.nsf/
    5cbcc578co1a . . . /Sutherland v Hatton.ht (accessed 12 February 2002).
Tehrani, N. (1997) Internal counselling provision for organizations, in
    M. Carroll and M. Walton (eds) *Handbook of Counselling In Organizations*.
    London: Sage.
Tehrani, N. (2001) Paper presented at the A Day in the Life of a Public Sector
    Employee Conference, Northampton, December.
Tudor, K. (1997) A complexity of contracts, in C. Sills (ed.) *Contracts In
    Counselling*. London: Sage.
Valentine, M. (1999) The cash nexus: or how the therapeutic fee is a form of
    communication, *British Journal of Psychotherapy*, 15(3): 346–54.
Ward, D. (2001) World heritage honour for revolutionary mills, *Guardian*,
    15 December.

Index

acclimatization process, 90–3
Addenbrookes NHS Trust, 38
addictive behaviour, 43–4
Adler, A., 27
ageing stages, 37–8
alcohol abuse organizations, 10–11
alcohol tests, 56–7
alienation, 5, 7, 27, 35, 57
collusion by counsellors, 131
Amaral, T.M., 69
American Counseling Association
    (ACA), 28
Code of Ethics and Practice, 54–5, 62
anxiety chain, 99–100, 102
Arthur, A., 68–9, 130
assessment
    form, 138–42a
    sessions, 29–30, 40, 106
Association for Counselling at Work
    (ACW), 23–4, 51, 52
audit, EAPs, 127–8
autonomy vs supervision, 116–17
Axelrod, S.D., 26–7

Bond, T., 54, 62, 83
Boots Company, 12–14
Bootshelp Service, 13–14
boundary issues, 47, 52–3
    organizational, 33, 63–4
Briner, R., 68
British Airways (BA) Crewcare, 17–19,
    42–3
British Association of Counselling and

Psychotherapy (BACP), 4, 23, 48
Ethical Framework, 53–4, 74
'multi-tasking', 63–4
Butler, C., 90–1

Cagney, T., 116
Carroll, M., 22–3, 73, 75, 98–9, 100,
    129, 134–5
and Walton, M., 3, 22, 57, 134
case management, 81–5, 118
caseload, 72, 88
Centre for Professional Employment
    Counselling (CEPEC), 23
Certified Employee Assistance
    Professional (CEAP), 24
childcare services, 36–7, 38
clients, 97–100, 110
    ex-clients, 63
Clinical Outcome in Routine
    Evaluation (CORE), 70–3
Clough, Rosemary, 11
cognitive-behavioural therapy (CBT),
    43–4
communication, 2
competitiveness, 124–5
confidentiality, 47, 50–1, 53–60, 126
    breaches, 59–60, 83
    ownership of client, 110
    physical setting, 53, 59, 77–80
    professional relationships, 104
    telephone counselling, 34–5
conflict resolution, 101, 135–6
conflict(s)

organization *vs* counsellor, 53–4, 56, 57–8, 91, 109–10
political values, 120
'triangle of conflict', 106–7
consultancy, 134–6
content skills, 112–13
contracts
    counsellor–organization, 98, 119
    EAPs, 110, 117–18
Cooper, C.L. and Highley-Marchington, J.C., 66–7, 70, 115–17
Cooper, J. and Alfille, H., 40
core conditions, 41–2
'corridor conversations', 80
counselling service
    reason for, 50–2
    see also employee assistance programmes (EAPs)
counter-transference, 39, 114–15
Court of Appeal, 50–2
Crewcare, British Airways (BA), 17–19, 42–3
crisis counselling, 44–5
Critical Incident and Recovery (CIPR), 44–5
Critical Incident Support, BA, 18–19
culture, organizational, 100–1, 128–9
Czander, W., 5–6

Darick, A.A., 55
Davidson, B.N. and Herlihy, P.A., 36, 37
debriefing, 44
'defensive transference', 89–90
definitions
    of counselling, 4, 27–8
    of workplace, 4
Diagnostic and Statistical Manual (DSM-III-R), 44
'Did Not Attend' (DNA) rates, 86
dogmatism, 127
drug tests, 56–7
dual relationships, 47, 53, 60–4
duty of care, 50–1

Egan, G., 18, 20–2, 27–8, 58, 108, 111, 112–13, 132, 133–4
Egan (Three Stage) model, 18, 20, 21, 42
eldercare service, 38
'emotional contagion', 68

empathy, 42, 43
Employee Assistance Professional Association (EAPA), 1, 10, 24–5, 131
    case management, 81–2
    competitiveness, 124–5
    evaluation guidelines, 69
    managerial referrals, 103
employee assistance programmes (EAPs), 1, 11, 81, 110
    absence of fee, 86, 88
    audit, 127–8
    confidentiality issues, 55, 56–7
    contracts, 117–18
    evaluation, 67, 68–9, 70
    external, 33–5, 43–4, 89, 98, 125
    ICAS, 18, 20, 33, 45
    information service, 32–3
    internal, 40, 63, 92–3, 98, 125
    introduction of, 33–5
    presenting problems, 31
    stress management, 130–1
    see also counselling service
employee–counsellor relationships, 97–100
employer–employee relationship, 2–3
evaluation, 47, 53, 64–75, 130–1
    form, 143–4*a*
    evidence from research, 67–8
    'evidence-based practice', 65, 70, 73
ex-clients, 63
external EAPs, 33–5, 43–4, 89, 98, 125

feedback, 73, 74, 75
Feltham, C., 3, 28, 124
financial issues
    advice, 33, 106
    competitiveness, 124–5
    EAP, 33–4, 60, 88
    fees *vs* free service, 85–90
    third party payments, 87–8
First Line Counselling, 16
Freud, S., 1, 4–6, 7, 36, 53, 64–5, 85, 122
    see also psychodynamic approach
Fromm, E., 6
Furnham, A., 6

Gabriel, L., 63–4
Gray, A., 53, 104
Greenson, R., 77, 89
grievance procedures, 92

group and individual psychology, 6, 7,
    52, 58

'Hawthorne effect', 9–10
'heads down' culture, 100–1
Health, Clara, 12
Hill, C., 128–30
Hirschorn, L., 52, 99, 100, 101, 102
historical overview, 2–4, 7–10
    see also welfarism
home–work balance, 35–8
Hood, V., 39–40
Hopkins, V., 136
humanistic approach, 41–3

'iceberg skills', 111, 114–15
ideological competitiveness, 124
Independent Counselling and Advisory
    Service (ICAS), 18, 20, 33, 45
individual and group psychology, 6, 7,
    52
industrial philanthropy, 7–8
information services, 32–3
internal EAPs, 40, 63, 92–3, 98, 125

Jenkins, P., 56
Jones, E., 5
judging by results, 130–1

Kelly, Eleanor, 12–13
Kets de Vries, M., 37
Kierkegaard, S., 94

Lago, C. and Kitchin, D., 103, 109, 110
Langs, R., 53, 79, 99
Leiper, R., 74–5
line managers, 108–15
listening, 26, 27
    states, 28
litigation issues, 50–2

McInnes, B., 51
McLellan, D., 7
McLeod, J., 27, 39, 43, 50, 62, 67–8,
    86, 115, 125
Malan, D., 53, 65, 106–7
management
    case, 81–5, 118
    relationships, 94–5, 108–15
    scientific, 8–9
    stress, 14, 130–1
    training, 111, 132–4

manager role, 111, 129–30, 132–4
managerial referrals, 103, 107
Marx, K. (Marxism), 5, 6–7, 27, 57
Mayo, E., 9
Mellor-Clark, J., 71, 72
    and Barkham, M., 72
    et al., 70–1
mentoring role, 92–3
Molnos, A., 52–3
'multi-tasking', 63–4
multiple roles, 92–3, 100–1, 127–30
Munro, R., 64
Munt, S., 82

National Health Service (NHS), 123,
    128, 130
    acclimatization, 91–2
    case management, 84
    containing environment, 110–11
    CORE system, 70–2, 73
    professional relationships, 96–7
    replacement of counsellors, 131
    vs EAP, 86–7
    work–life balance policy, 38
North Staffordshire Combined NHS
    Healthcare Trust Staff Counselling
    Service, 29–31
    assessment form, 138–42a
    evaluation form, 143–4a
    presenting problems, 31–2
Northamptonshire Constabulary,
    16–17

O'Carroll, L., 66
Oher, J., 69
    et al., 31
organization(s), 6
    boundary issues, 33, 63–4
    consultants, 134–6
    contracts, 98, 119
    –counsellor relationship, 118–20
    culture, 100–1, 128–9
    life span of counsellors, 95–6
    procedures/policies, 92–3
    selection of counsellors, 48–50
    vs counselling conflicts, 53–4, 56,
        57–8, 91, 109–10
    see also professional relationships
outcomes of counselling, 28
    see also evaluation

Palmer, B., 135–6

Paproski, D. and Haverkamp, B., 104–5
Parlett, M. and Page, F., 20
pedantry, 127
physical setting(s), 53, 59, 77–81
pioneers of workplace counselling,
 19–25
Police Federation, 16–17
political values, 120
Post Office, 14–16
post-traumatic stress disorder (PTSD),
 44
presenting problems, 31–2
process skills, 112
professional relationships
 EAP, 115–18
 employees/clients, 97–100
 line manager, 108–15
 multiple, 106–8
 referral dynamics, 102–8
 senior management, 94–5
psychiatric referrals, 103–4, 105
psychiatric/psychological injury, 50–1,
 52
psychodynamic approach, 39–41
 see also Freud, S.

records/notes, 78
recruitment/selection, 48–50, 83, 116
Reddy, M., 19–20, 57, 105–6
redundancies, counsellor, 131
referral dynamics, 102–8
research see entries beginning evidence
resistance, 57–8
 case management, 82–3
 evaluation, 66–7, 72–3
 referral, 105–6
Robinson, S., 66
Rogers, C., 41–2, 43

scientific management, 8–9
Scott, M. and Stradling, S., 44
secret relationship, 57–8
selection/recruitment, 48–50, 83, 116
self-referral, 102–3, 106
senior management, 94–5
sessions
 assessment, 29–30, 40, 106
 number, 39–40, 41, 84, 87, 88–90
setting(s), 53, 59, 77–81
social stigma of counselling, 3–4
Sonnenstuhl, W., 8–10, 99, 102–3, 116,
 117

and Trice, H.M., 7, 8, 95
Steele, D.P., 10, 11
 and Trice, H., 11
stress management, 14, 130–1
stress-related injury, 50–1, 52
supervision vs autonomy, 116–17
supply and demand, 131
system dynamics, 119–20
systemic approach, 113–14

Tavistock Consultancy Service (TCS),
 114, 133, 135–6
'Tavistock paradigm', 135–6
Taylor, F.W. ('Taylorism'), 8–9
'team development', 135
Tehrani, N., 14–16, 134
telephone counselling, 34–5
theoretical approaches, 38–45
therapeutic framework, 53
third party
 payments, 87–8
 referrals, 103–4
Three Stage (Egan) model, 18, 20, 21,
 42
trade unions, 8, 10, 11, 32
 counsellor membership, 120
training
 counselling, 111
 management, 111, 132–4
transactional analysis (TA), 20, 98
transference, 39, 40–1, 106–7
 counter-transference, 39, 114–15
 'defensive transference', 89–90
 'triangle of conflict/person', 106–7
Tudor, K., 98

United Kingdom (UK), 1, 3, 7–8, 10,
 11, 38
 EAPA, 24–5, 69, 81–2
 'evidence-based practice', 65, 70
United States (US), 1, 3, 7, 8, 10–11, 36
 EAPA, 24, 131

visibility of counsellor, 96–7

Ward, D., 8
welfare officers, 12–13, 14–15
welfarism, 9–11
 and development of counselling,
 11–19
Western Electric (Hawthorne studies),
 9–10

women employees
   and welfare officers, 12–13
   work–life balance, 36, 38
Wood, Mary, 11–12
work

   concepts of, 4–7
   performance, 68–9
work–home balance, 35–8
workaholism, 35–6
workplace, definitions, 4

ON TRAINING TO BE A THERAPIST
THE LONG AND WINDING ROAD TO QUALIFICATION

John Karter

Having become aware during his own training of the enormous and varied pressures that students of psychotherapy and counselling have to face, often without any real source of support, the author seeks to explore the professional and personal difficulties, anxieties, emotions and pitfalls engendered by this unique and often destabilizing process from what he terms a 'student's eye view'.

Trainees frequently feel overwhelmed by an exhausting round of studying, clinical placements, supervision, and personal therapy, and are often engaged in a juggling act between training, family and work. The fundamental objective of the book is to confront and to ameliorate these demands and difficulties and to highlight the fact that therapy training can and should be an enjoyable and fulfilling process in itself.

Among the many issues looked at are the ways in which training can change us as people, how it can affect our personal relationships, the dangers of adhering too strictly to theory, the terrors of essay writing, difficult issues with clients such as unplanned contact and sexuality, making the most of supervision, personal therapy, and many more.

On Training to be a Therapist has been designed for use as a standard text on training courses at all levels. It is aimed principally at psychotherapy and counselling students, but will also appeal to qualified practitioners, tutors and supervisors looking for a different perspective.

Contents
Foreword – Introduction – Facing up to mission impossible – A change for the better? – The art of survival on the long and winding road – The dangers in playing it by the book – Super-vision syndrome and how to avoid it – Caution: slow go area ahead – Up close and personal – The bitter-sweet taste of freedom – Bibliography – Index.

176pp   0 335 21001 5 (Paperback)   0 335 21002 3 (Hardback)

VALUES AND ETHICS IN THE PRACTICE OF PSYCHOTHERAPY AND COUNSELLING

Fiona Palmer Barnes and Lesley Murdin

The work of every school of psychotherapy and every therapist is inevitably structured by a value system and requires codes of ethics and practice. This book addresses the conscious and unconscious aspects of the value system in which therapists are situated. *Values and Ethics in the Practice of Psychotherapy and Counselling* explores the central issues through the experience of the contributors, each of whom is well known in this field. Each chapter will raise questions for the reader which will stimulate individual thinking about practice or can form a basis for discussion and debate for training or graduate groups. The book is firmly rooted in practice. Each chapter deals with a different aspect of the psychotherapist's work beginning with the general underlying principles, continuing through matters of technique and on to contextual issues. Finally the book moves to the outer world, politics and spirituality as ways of connecting inner and outer, social and individual. The arrangement of chapters allows for flexibility and creativity while providing a coherent structure.

Values and Ethics in the Practice of Psychotherapy and Counselling is recommended reading for psychotherapists, psychoanalysts and counsellors in training and practice.

Contents
Foreword – Introduction – Ethical principles – Psychotherapy as the practice of ethics – Responsible involvement: ethical dimensions of collegial responsibility – Assessment: for what? for whom? – Erotics and ethics: the passionate dilemmas of the therapeutic couple – Ethics and values in our practice: impasse in psychotherapy and organizations – Success and failure – Values and ethics in researching psychotherapy – Complexities of practice: psychotherapy in the real world – The sanctum, the citadel and the souk: confidentiality and paradox – The private face and the public face of psychotherapy – Beyond psychotherapy: beyond ethics? – And if not now, when?: spirituality, psychotherapy and politics – Index.

240pp   0 335 20475 9 (Paperback)   0 335 20476 7 (Hardback)